Radical Happiness

Radical Happiness

A Guide to Awakening

GINA LAKE

Endless Satsang Foundation

Endless Satsang Foundation

www.radicalhappiness.com

Cover art: © Sugatha S. Roeder, "Passionate Heart." For more information, please visit www.flowermandala.com.

First Edition 2005
Second Edition 2007

ISBN for this edition: 978-0-6151-5394-0

CONTENTS

PREFACE

I came to write this book after being a new age seeker, teacher, channel, writer, and astrologer for fifteen years and then finally discovering Advaita and satsang. Along the way, I met many seekers. Some were looking for happiness and a way to improve their lives, while others were looking for the Truth, no matter what sacrifice it might demand, including the ultimate one: the self, or the ego.

I have to admit that I became a seeker because I wanted a better, happier, more successful *me*; and the spiritual path—the new age paradigm in particular—offered some hope for that. New age teachings claim that we create our reality, and they seemed to promise that if I thought the right thoughts, I could get whatever I wanted.

Something inside me knew better and wasn't willing to settle for having my desires fulfilled, if that was even possible. This something brought me to my teacher, Adyashanti, when I was finally ready to hear the truth: I don't exist! Suddenly, the point of the spiritual path became clear. It was not about improving myself, but discovering the truth about who I am. That was what I really wanted. I wanted the Truth.

Several years have passed since then, and during that time I have been married to an Advaita teacher, Nirmala. *Advaita* is a Sanskrit word that means *non-dual* and refers to a philosophy that points to our essential oneness with everything. As my own understanding ripened, I felt a pull to write again, and this book is the result.

As it was being written, I began to see it is a bridge between new age/metaphysical beliefs, including some of the ideas that have been channeled by myself and others over the past few decades, and non-dual philosophy, particularly the philosophy spoken about in satsang. Satsang is what my husband and other teachers like him call the form of teaching they do.

Satsang is a Sanskrit word that means "gathering for the Truth." In satsang, people gather with a teacher to discover who they really are. In Advaita, the question, Who am I? is asked as a means of stripping away all ideas related to the personal self and coming to a realization of the Emptiness, the Awareness, the Nothingness that we are.

Radical Happiness could not have been written without the influence of everyone I have known as well as the help of many unseen helpers, who are guiding each of us Home. More than ever, I am aware that what we do is only possible because it is part of a collective effort on the part of those in both the seen and unseen worlds.

A few of my helpers have been so obviously instrumental in making this book possible that I have to take a moment to thank them here:

Nirmala, you are the love of my life and my greatest blessing. I look forward to continuing our journey of love and discovery. I am most deeply grateful for your unwavering affection and support. I have never experienced being accepted and loved so steadily by anyone before, and it is an amazing gift. The wisdom that has come through you is reflected throughout this book.

Adyashanti, I feel so blessed that you entered my life. With only a few words, you cut through my many misunderstandings and catapulted me into a new life.

I would also like to thank my twin brother, Tom, for his limitless love and support. You have made my life so much easier, and what you have done for me has given me the freedom and opportunity to sit down and write this book.

G.L.
April 2005

INTRODUCTION

Happiness doesn't need to be sought because it isn't hidden. It's like a treasure you have always had but never realized you had. True happiness—radical happiness—is the happiness that is always present and not dependent on circumstances. It's not the happiness that comes from getting what you want, but the happiness that comes from wanting what is here now. It comes from realizing that who you *think* you are, that is, who your thoughts tell you that you are, isn't who you really are. True happiness comes from experiencing your true nature by being present in each moment.

Your thoughts about yourself create a false self, an imaginary self, that seems real. The false self, or *ego*, is made up of beliefs, opinions, judgments, memories, fantasies, hopes, dreams, fears, and other conditioning. The ego is experienced mentally as thoughts about ourselves and about everything else. The term *egoic mind* has been used throughout this book to refer to the aspect of the mind that is an expression of the ego. The egoic mind is the voice in your head, the ongoing commentary that the mind engages in. This voice is the voice of the ego, or false self. The egoic mind creates an imaginary reality that most of us live in. It's also the source of unhappiness and suffering.

There is another aspect of the mind, apart from the egoic mind, which could be called the functional, or practical, mind. This is the aspect of the mind we use to read, calculate, and do other mental work. It doesn't talk to us like the egoic mind does;

it's simply a tool we pick up and use when we need it. That aspect of the mind is not a problem and doesn't cause suffering. It is enjoyable and a useful tool for living.

The ego isn't wise. The ego is only conditioning and other programming that give us a sense of being somebody. The ego, through the egoic mind, attempts to run our life, but it's a poor master. It leads us in directions that promise happiness but don't deliver. Pursuing the ego's hopes, dreams, and ideas about ourselves and life, instead of resulting in happiness, has only taken us farther away from the true source of happiness, which is who we really are, who we are beyond our thoughts about ourselves. This is a radical perspective: To realize the peace and happiness that have always been here, we have to be willing to see that who we thought we were has never been anything more than thoughts, and that those thoughts aren't good guides for how to live.

Happiness has never been available in the things we think will give us happiness. The happiness from achieving some desire is always fleeting and never fully satisfying. And yet we tend to believe that if we just get a little more of what we desire or if we desire the right thing, we will finally be happy. This belief is exactly what keeps us from realizing that happiness is already here.

Happiness is here, now, and finding true happiness is only a matter of realizing that. It's here in the experience of our true self, which is what is actually living this life. However, as long as we are entranced by the egoic mind and its ideas about *me* and desires of something better, we won't notice the peace, joy, and contentment that are available in this simple moment through the experience of our true nature.

Radical Happiness explains the process of waking up out of identification with the egoic mind and what it's like to live in alignment with our true nature. This process of dis-identification is called *awakening*. The exercises that are offered throughout invite you to look more deeply and apply the information more personally. They will help you unmask the ego and discover who you really are and, in the process, discover true happiness.

I invite you to suspend all your ideas about who you are and what you need to be happy, and to look with curiosity at who you really are. What is this mystery that is you? And is there really anything you need to be happy?

CHAPTER 1
The Illusion of Separation

DIVINE PLAY

Everything that exists is an expression of one Being, which is referred to by countless names: God, Oneness, the Self, Essence, the Divine, the Source, the Beloved, and so many others. We are the Oneness, but it seems like we are separate from it. The ego is this sense of being a separate individual with certain beliefs, opinions, judgments, desires, dreams, fears, feelings, and other programming, or conditioning.

The ego is really nothing but a set of ideas or perceptions we label *me*. Who are you, the personality, other than ideas or perceptions about yourself? You might say that you are a body, but that's obviously not an adequate description. When you think of yourself, you may think of your body, but even those are just thoughts about your body.

That sense of separation and of being a *me* is created by the Oneness, the Self, our true nature, as a means for playing in and exploring this physical reality. This world is all divine play, *lila*, as the Hindu mystics say, a way for the Self to experience what it couldn't experience any other way. The Self hides from itself in this world with the intent of finding itself again. The Self becomes deeply immersed in illusion, the illusion of being a separate individual, so that it can explore life as these many individual forms, which allow the Self to have an enormous range of experiences.

Anything the Self imagines, it can experience not only in this reality, but also in others. Our particular reality has certain parameters within which it explores, while other realities have others. The possibilities are as limitless as the divine imagination. When we are in touch with our true nature, we feel the Self's joy in exploring whatever we are experiencing, which is not like any other experience the Self has ever had. That joy is what permeates every moment of life, which is where the happiness we all seek lies, right here in the simplest moment. It is inherent in life, natural and innate to it. It couldn't be otherwise.

Since the Self wishes to fully involve itself in the illusion of being a separate individual, it has programmed each of us to feel we exist as separate individuals. That is the setup of the drama being played out in this realm. Through us, the Self wishes to experience every possible blissful and terrible experience, but it also wishes to awaken from the dream/nightmare because that is also part of the drama. It's an heroic story: The Self differentiates into form again and again, accepts challenges, learns from them, and eventually rediscovers itself.

The ego plays an important role in this drama. It is the protagonist, complete with beliefs, desires, drives, talents, and shortcomings. It also plays the antagonist by creating challenges and suffering. In the drama we call life, we experience ourselves as the star, with others playing supporting roles. This sense of being the center of the universe is true of every ego. Meanwhile, life is happening all around us. Other people's lives and their dramas, with their dreams and desires and drives, collide unpredictably, creating an ever-changing situation that either delivers what we want or not. This is how the ego sees life. Its narrow point of view is based on how life is going for *me* at any one time.

SELF-REALIZATION

The Self is equally involved and interested in the playing out of the ego's drama, but it is interested not only for the experience and learning that the drama affords, but also because it intends to awaken from the illusion of separation someday. Waking up out of illusion and the realization that we are the Self rather than a separate individual is called *self-realization*, or *awakening*, and waking up can happen suddenly or slowly. The Self intends not only to awaken, but also to express itself more fully through each of us. Its goal is not only for us to realize our true nature as the Self, but also for us to act accordingly. This acting as the Self is sometimes referred to as *embodiment*. Once we awaken, we begin to embody the Self more fully.

Some people are born self-realized, but even they usually go through a period of ego-dominance before they awaken and self-realization is regained. When someone realizes the Self, we say they have awakened because self-realization is like waking up from a dream into a new reality, one that is richer, freer, and not dominated by the egoic mind and its false beliefs.

Self-realization is possible for anyone, but only a few are interested in waking up from the dream. Most are enjoying it in their own way, and questioning it hasn't occurred to them. However, eventually the time comes to wake up, and when it does, there is a deep longing to discover the truth about our existence. The ego's drives, desires, and drama recede, and more attention and energy are given to the Self, as it begins to move more through us.

Turning away from the ego and its desires and perceptions toward the Self is a huge step in our evolution. It is a coming of age as a human being, for our destiny is to awaken from the egoic state and discover that we are divine. That discovery forever changes the experience of life, as love replaces fear as the driving force. We long to experience the deepest kind of love.

Upon awakening, the locus of our identity shifts from the ego to the Self. Before awakening, the sense of *me* is associated with our personality, our body, and the ego, which includes our thoughts, beliefs, desires, feelings, roles, identities, and other conditioning. After awakening, we know ourselves as the Self, which we see as expressing itself through our particular personality and body. This shift can often be seen in the eyes of those who have awakened.

When self-realization happens suddenly, it is unmistakable because the change of identity is so obvious. When it happens slowly over time, the shift is subtler and less dramatic and sometimes goes unnoticed. Many who are awake don't know it. They also don't care. They don't see themselves as special, but very ordinary because self-realization is such an ordinary and unremarkable state.

Self-realization is our natural state, so self-realization feels like coming home. Rather than being extraordinary, our natural state is very simple and peaceful, uncomplicated by all the problem-creation of the egoic mind. Thoughts and feelings still arise, but they are understood to be part of the egoic self. They seem impersonal, as if they belong to someone else.

This objectivity toward thoughts and feelings isn't dry and lifeless, however, but full of curiosity and love. Objectivity makes it easier to be intimate with our thoughts and feelings, to give them the attention and love they need to evolve. It actually allows us to be more fully engaged with life rather than distancing us from life because it lacks any kind of judgment. From this perspective, our conditioning seems sweet and endearing instead of true and compelling.

For most, self-realization continues to deepen over time. It is common to be drawn back into ego-identification temporarily by pockets of remaining conditioning. When that happens, we feel caught in suffering again, but the experience is different after awakening because we know we aren't the egoic self that is suffering. After awakening, although we can still become identified with the ego, we never totally forget who we really are; so identification isn't as strong, and it doesn't last as long.

It's very rare for conditioning to completely drop away after awakening. It's so rare that this is more of a myth. This and other myths about self-realization cause a lot of confusion for spiritual seekers, who often expect awakening to look very different than it does. Many think their problems will disappear after awakening, and some problems do. But the usual problems of being human remain—bodies still get sick, loved ones die, and accidents happen—only now, these things aren't seen as problems, but just what *is*, what happens to be showing up now.

Our problems are created by the mind, which tends to define however things are as a problem. After awakening, this kind of problem-generation stops (or isn't given attention), and that results in a much simpler experience of life. After all, once the mind has identified a problem, it doesn't stop there; it dreams up ways to fix it and then mobilizes the body in that direction. Much of our time and energy is spent trying to solve imaginary problems instead of living the life we are meant to live, which is a life full of joy and love, not problems.

For example, you might decide that the way you look isn't good enough to attract a mate—that's a problem. So you buy new clothes, restyle your hair, work out, and go on a diet. But is that premise true? Does love really require all that effort?

After awakening, we are very comfortable in our skin. We are comfortable with the way things are. We love life, and we love the varied expressions of it: fat, thin, beautiful, ugly, Black, White, young, old. We don't have ideas of what someone should look like. Whatever they look like is what they should look like. Whatever life is right now is what life should be. We embrace the diversity, the ever-changing-ness, and the unpredictability of life. We accept whatever is—and not just accept it, but love it.

Imagine what that would be like. Peace and love are really all any of us wants, to be totally in love and at peace with whatever is. So how attractive do you think someone who loves everything is? Do you think he or she would need the right clothes, car, or hair to be loved?

CONDITIONING

Before awakening, we live our lives largely in response to our conditioning. After awakening, this changes. Our conditioning is our own particular set of ideas and beliefs about life that determine, for the most part, how we will act in a certain situation. If only conditioning were uncomplicated and trustworthy, it might be an adequate guide to living; but because it is contradictory and mistaken, it's a poor guide. Conditioning comes from many different sources and was, for the most part, unquestioned by those sources; so although certain ideas and beliefs may have stood the test of time, they may not be true or relevant today, or at least not true for *this* moment.

Aside from useful admonishments and practical advice, such as "Be nice" and "Brush your teeth twice a day," conditioning is often ideas about how things *should* be, such as, "The weather should be sunny if you're going on a picnic." Our minds are filled with ideas about how things should and shouldn't be. And how we suffer when our ideas don't match reality! Even a small thing, like a lack of sunshine, can seem like a problem; and because we can't change the situation, we feel sad or angry. Without the belief that picnics have to have sunshine to turn out well, we wouldn't feel sad or angry over a lack of sunshine. Sunshine or a lack of it has nothing to do with our potential for happiness, but our conditioning, what we believe, *does*.

Actually, our conditioning isn't the cause of our suffering as much as our relationship to it: how much we believe it. If we don't give our attention to our thoughts about how things supposedly *should* be, it doesn't matter if that conditioning is there or not. Our conditioning has only as much influence over us as we allow it to have.

Most of our thoughts reflect conditioning acquired from others. Our conditioning tells us how life is and how it should be. It tells us what is good and bad, right and wrong, pretty and ugly. It tells us what to believe about God and religion, men and women, cats and dogs, and anything else that can be named. Our conditioning tells us how to behave and what to think and do in certain situations. When we are young, we accept these ideas without questioning them. It's enough that those who have authority over us have sanctioned these ideas. Those we are dependent upon are identified with these ideas, so we identify with these ideas. When we are young, it really can't be any other way.

We need conditioning. We can't do without it. It's part of life. It provides a structure from which to function in the world. Those who were given truer and more positive conditioning have an easier time than those with less true and more negative conditioning. We all have conditioning; the question is how well it serves us as adults, now that we are capable of evaluating it.

As adults, we can choose to pay attention to our conditioning or not, and we can replace our beliefs with ones that work better. As adults, we can take control over what we believe in a way that wasn't possible as children. Children are at the mercy of their conditioning, but adults aren't, although we may feel like we still are.

Therapy has to do with sorting through conditioning, keeping what is helpful, ignoring what is not, and adopting more positive conditioning. This is work, but it is important work and something that must be done if we are to fulfill our potential.

Exercise: Becoming Aware of Conditioning

This inquiry is especially useful when you are feeling bad about yourself, someone else, or your situation. It can help you uncover the conditioning (mistaken beliefs and assumptions) behind your unhappiness.

What is arising in your mind right now? Where did it come from? Someone? Something you read? Something you were taught? Is it true? Is it useful in this moment? Practice being aware of your thoughts. What thoughts are practical and useful, and what thoughts are not?

THE LANGUAGE OF THE SELF

The problem with conditioning is it often interferes with paying attention to our intuition, which is how the Self communicates its plan and inspiration to us. Intuition operates in everyone to some extent, but we are more able to hear and respond to it when our conditioning is held more lightly. When we follow our intuition instead of our conditioning, the potential for happiness is so much greater. A life lived in response to conditioning is dry and full of doubt, shame, guilt, unworthiness, fear, and self-hatred.

If our conditioning is more fortunate, following it can result in success through hard work, positive relationships, and the satisfaction of struggling and overcoming obstacles. But there is more to life than accomplishments. It is possible to feel successful and have positive relationships without so much struggle and effort. Following our intuition leads to creativity and unique expression, and it lends ease to life, as well as fulfillment and deep satisfaction unparalleled by any worldly satisfaction.

After awakening, we don't listen to conditioning as much as to an inner voice, an intuitive one, that offers direct guidance for every moment. Conditioning, on the other hand, is merely a set of formulas and rules for behavior, and what good are those when they fail miserably at times? We need intuition to know when and how to apply those formulas and rules, if at all, to the present moment.

Fortunately, thoughts and intuitions are easy to distinguish. Unlike thoughts, intuitions don't register in the mind, but more in the body, particularly in the center of the chest and the gut. They feel more like a knowing, a yes, about what to do. Thoughts, on the other hand, are often connected to a mental voice, a voice in our head, which may seem like our own voice or that of a parent or some other authority figure.

THOUGHTS AND THE *ME* THOUGHT

Unlike intuitions, thoughts are clearly located in the mind. Although they may have some wisdom to them, for the most part, our thoughts are stabs at truth and tell us little about how to live in the present moment. Instead, thoughts keep us at arm's length from the moment. They keep us living in a mentally fabricated reality, the realm of ideas, instead of in the present moment. Thoughts from the egoic mind interfere with life instead of enhancing it.

The truth about our thoughts runs contrary to our deeply held belief that our thoughts are important and meaningful. Somehow, we've been convinced of this instead of seeing the truth—that our thoughts keep us from reality and from being present in the moment. Our conviction that thoughts from the egoic mind are necessary, true, and meaningful guides for life is part of the illusion and what helps hold the illusion in place.

Thoughts are the structure of the ego and what maintain it. Without thoughts, the ego wouldn't exist. The belief that thoughts are important, valuable, and meaningful is the lynchpin that, when removed, causes the whole game to fall apart; and where we land is smack dab in reality, in this alive moment.

Aside from conditioned ideas and beliefs, thoughts are largely about the past and the future. It's obvious how our thoughts about the past and future keep us from the present moment, even if it's less clear how other thoughts do. When we are thinking about the past or the future, we are mentally reconstructing images of the past and the future and seeing ourselves in them.

Who is it you see in the past or future? Isn't what you see just an idea of you? In those images of the past or future, you see yourself at a distance, as if you were viewing the entire scene. Meanwhile, who are you really? You are not this thought of yourself in the past or the future, but for the time being, you are identified with it, just as you become identified with a character in a movie.

While that is going on, you no longer are in touch with what's going on in the moment, with the sensations and the experience of the moment. Instead, the moment has been covered over by thoughts of some other moment in time. The present moment still exists, but it's not being experienced purely, simply.

A part of us doesn't want to experience life purely and simply: the ego. It wouldn't exist without the mental drama it creates. It exists and thrives on thoughts about the past and plans of the future. It constantly mulls over the story of me: "How's it going for me?" "How am I going to do?" "How did I do?" "What do I have to do to get things to go my way?" Evaluations and plans are the stuff the ego feeds on, which cause it to loom large in our consciousness, blocking out awareness of other aspects of reality. When we live in the egoic state of consciousness, life is about the story and how it's going, and all the worries, fears, concerns, and problems entailed in that. That is the ongoing drama the ego is engrossed in.

However, there is another life living itself under or behind or beyond all that drama, and that is reality. Reality is unfolding beautifully moment by moment, and it allows the ego's drama to take center stage as long as it will. Eventually, the ego's drama will get old, and reality will break through, and we will choose reality over the ego's entrancements. That point in our evolution is the beginning of a new awareness and a new willingness to realize the Self.

Many lifetimes are spent immersed in the egoic state of consciousness and its lessons. These are important lessons that the Self willingly embraces for the unique experiences they provide. The Self is curious and wishes to explore every experience, even limited and unfulfilling ones. It has no problem with being involved in the egoic state of consciousness. The Self chooses to explore egoic consciousness for a time, but it also chooses to wake up from it. Everyone will awaken in one lifetime or another. Then reality, which has been there all along, will be seen in its purity.

In the meantime, the ego, the *me*, appears to exist, although it actually only exists as a thought. It appears the ego is having thoughts, but the ego, itself, is a thought. The ego seems very real, and yet it has no substance. If you look very closely, you see that the ego is composed of thoughts about *me*, and nothing more.

Furthermore, those thoughts about *me* are constantly changing, so the idea *me* is not even stable or continuous: One moment you are clever and the next moment you are not. Your ideas about yourself are always changing. Take your self-image, for instance: You look different in your mind's eye from one day to the next, depending on who you are comparing yourself to or what other ideas or beliefs are moving through your mind.

Exercise: Examining the "I" Thought

This inquiry will help you see who you really are and who you are not.

Who or what is the I that you imagine yourself to be? When you say "I," what do you imagine? What thoughts and images make up the I? Is the I the same throughout your life or even throughout your day? Have you always imagined and talked about yourself in the same way?

How hard is it, really, to change the description and images that go along with I? Isn't it only a matter of exchanging thoughts and images for other thoughts and images? How difficult is that? Is the I who you are? Who is it that is able to think about the I? Could that be who you really are?

The mind is primarily the instrument of the ego, since so much of our thinking is an attempt to get the ego what it wants. Nevertheless, it can also be the instrument of the Self. Occasionally, thoughts instead of the intuition are the vehicle for communicating the Self's inspiration and plan. When thoughts from the Self appear in the mind, they ring of truth and are accompanied by excitement, happiness, relaxation, and mental clarity. On the other hand, thoughts that come from the ego and have little truth to them are accompanied by mental confusion, energetic contraction, and tenseness in the body. Whether a thought results in expansion and peace or contraction and tension is how we can tell how true a particular thought is and where it is coming from.

In addition to serving the ego, the mind also helps us balance a checkbook, draw a blueprint, read a map, evaluate possible escape routes from danger, and do a myriad of other mental tasks. We need the mind to function, but it is also full of useless and incorrect information, conditioning, that passes as facts. We need the aspect of the mind that allows us to do mental work, but we don't actually need the egoic mind to function.

Self-realization entails a certain mastery of the mind that includes being aware of our thoughts and being able to discriminate between ones that have some truth and usefulness and ones that don't. This takes some practice, but most of all, it takes sensitivity to the signs that something is true or false. Not only do we need to be aware of our thoughts, but also of their impact on us energetically, mentally, and emotionally. Here is an exercise that will help you notice the effect your thoughts have on you:

Exercise: Exploring the Effect and Truth of Your Thoughts

This inquiry will help you become aware of how your thinking affects your state of consciousness. It also gives you a means for telling how true your thoughts are.

What are you thinking right now and how does it affect you? Does it make you feel expanded or contracted? Some thoughts cause us to become more contracted and ego-identified, while others cause us to become more expanded and aligned with the Self. Those that do the latter could be said to be truer than the former. This is because truth puts us in touch with Truth, or reality, while what is not true puts us in touch with what is not real: the ego.

No matter how hard we try, we can't control the coming and going of thoughts. They come out of nowhere and disappear into nowhere. Spiritual seekers, in particular, often feel discouraged because they have certain thoughts they don't want to have. Everyone has thoughts they would rather not have. This is part of the human condition, which includes having a mind that has been conditioned, or programmed.

BECOMING AWARE OF YOUR THOUGHTS

Although we can't control our thoughts, we *can* learn to become more aware of them. This may seem like a simple thing, but becoming aware of our thoughts is a very big step in evolution. It requires dis-identification from the egoic mind, which is why it is such a big step. When we aren't aware of our thoughts, we are likely to be identified with them, and therefore identified with the ego, and we are likely to respond automatically to them, without questioning them. Doing that results in a lot of suffering and more difficulties than necessary because the ego isn't a very wise master.

When we are identified with the egoic mind, we believe we are who we think we are: our self-image and the labels we have for ourselves. But is that who you are? If that is who you are, then who is it that is able to think about this question? What is it that is aware of the ideas that make up your self-image? What is it that is aware of the coming and going of thoughts?

This idea *me* may seem to reside in the body or the mind or both, but what is it that's aware of the body and the mind? Could that be who you are, and the body and the mind are just functioning within that awareness? In that case, would you be limited to just the body and mind, or could you actually be anything you are aware of right now? Could all of it be you? What if that were true? What would that mean? Life would be lived from a very different place.

These questions can wake you up out of the egoic state of consciousness. Questioning the assumptions of the egoic mind is a very powerful tool for awakening. Becoming aware of the egoic mind, its thoughts, and their truth or falseness can help us bust through the web of illusion cast by the egoic mind, which fools us into thinking we are separate, when we aren't. Becoming more aware of the egoic mind can also free us from the suffering that the ego's mistaken beliefs and perceptions cause.

Exercise: Who Am I?

This inquiry will help you disentangle your identity from the false self and experience your true nature. You may only need a moment to remember who you are. At other times, you may want to spend several minutes asking these questions.

What are you aware of right now? If you are aware of a thought, ask: "Who or what is aware of this thought?" If you are aware of a feeling, ask: "Who or what is aware of this feeling?" If you are aware of a sensation, ask: "Who or what is aware of this sensation?"

The tendency is to become identified with the thought, feeling, or sensation and lose awareness of our true nature, which is pure Awareness. The purpose of these questions, this inquiry, is not to come up with answers, but to point you to the experience of who you are. If you find yourself thinking about the answers, go back to the questions and stay with the *experience* that the questions lead you to, which is an experience of not knowing instead of knowing. The real you is there in the not-knowing.

THE REASONS FOR DIS-IDENTIFYING FROM THE EGO

Dis-identification from the ego is a natural step in our evolution, and it also has one very big advantage: Suffering and problems disappear. Suffering is caused by the ego wanting life to be other than the way it is. And problems are created by defining something as a problem, and there is only one thing that does that: the ego. Detaching from the ego and aligning with our true nature means an end to suffering and problems.

Although the ego pretends to be able to guide us toward happiness, the ego is actually the cause of unhappiness. Identification with it is an experience of unhappiness, contraction, discontentment, restlessness, lack of acceptance, striving desiring, and the full range of negative feelings. This describes the human condition for the most part. When we are no longer identified with the ego and, instead, aligned with the Self, we experience true happiness, relaxation, expansion, peace, contentment, love, compassion, acceptance, gratitude, and wisdom, all the things we so long for when we are lost in ego-identification but don't know how to get. Furthermore, alignment with the Self makes it possible to fulfill our life purpose and move more easily through life.

Once we see the truth about the ego and choose to not identify with it, it's possible to be happy and at peace with life. What makes that happiness and peace possible is what has always been here and living this life—the Self—which is exquisitely content with its creation.

CHAPTER 2
Waking Up from the Illusion

THE SPIRITUAL PATH

Life is a game of hide and seek that the Self is playing with itself. It hides in the illusion of being an individual so that it can discover itself again. Meanwhile, it enjoys the drama and play of being an individual, a character, until the game is done. When that game is finished, is not only up to the Self, but also up to the one who is lost in illusion. We have to realize we are caught in illusion and begin to try to find the way out before the Self shows us the way. An element of free will is at play in awakening, although the stage is often set and the plot designed with the elements necessary to evoke awakening. Still, we must be willing to question the illusion.

The willingness to question life is often accompanied by a weariness of the drama, either because the suffering has become too great or because the drama has lost its allure. The baubles the ego offers no longer satisfy a deeper longing for a more permanent happiness. A spiritual longing develops that energizes the first step of the journey Home.

The spiritual path is essentially the path to awakening, but the journey of consciousness doesn't end at awakening. After awakening, consciousness continues to unfold in its own way and in its own time. Everyone has a different experience of awakening and what follows. Nevertheless, certain patterns emerge in this unfolding of consciousness.

AFTER AWAKENING

An awakening is often followed by a honeymoon period, when an expanded state of consciousness is experienced more or less continuously. Feelings of great freedom, elation, or Oneness may last days or weeks or months. How long that honeymoon period lasts varies greatly from person to person, as does what comes after that period.

After awakening, many also experience mental disorientation, physical aches and pains, or illness because the body and energy field need to make adjustments to the awakened state. Mentally, the experience can be one of lethargy, feeling lost in space, not being able to move or function, and detachment from any sense of self.

At some point after awakening, most people experience some degree of spiritual inflation. The ego re-forms around "I am awake" and takes some pride and sense of superiority in that. This phase is pretty apparent, if not to the newly awakened person, to those around him or her. There's often a tendency to talk about the awakening, to wonder who else is and is not awake, and to identify oneself as awake to others. An identity forms around being awake. This identification can be rather harmless, but if the person doesn't realize the ego has taken on spiritual garb, this phase can last for some time.

One of the most dramatic results of awakening is the dropping away of much of our former conditioning. Many of our old beliefs, ideas, and self-images no longer show up in the mind. We understand them to have been the trappings of the character we played.

And yet we are still here in the world, in the same body, and usually in the same roles: If you were a mother before awakening, you are still a mother. If you were a husband, you are still a husband. If you were a carpenter, you are probably still a carpenter. But in the midst of our roles and situations, we are different. We respond more naturally because our mind is less cluttered by ideas about how to behave and who we are. We respond now to what is needed in the moment, instead of to our ideas about what should happen.

We don't believe many of our old ideas anymore, and they just don't interest us. We don't spend time thinking about what we did or what we will do because that is clearly irrelevant now. It doesn't matter. Before, we thought it made a difference. Now we see that our thinking has never been anything but impotent and that the *me* has never been anything but another flimsy idea that has no reality.

This is a relief, but it's also disorienting to be in the world without our usual beliefs, goals, and desires to be somebody. Once we see that we are both nobody and everybody, we can't be bothered with trying to be somebody anymore. It's clear now that all our life we have just been role-playing, and playing this character just isn't interesting anymore.

But what takes the place of playing this character? It can take a while, often years, before we move fully into functioning from the awakened state. So during this period, we may still go back to our conditioned ideas about how to behave. We often feel a sense of loss or emptiness in being without our old familiar goals, self-images, and rules for behavior. Before awakening, we knew who we were and what we wanted and where we were trying to go. Now we don't. We are nobody with nowhere to go, and any remnant of ego remaining will find that empty and unfulfilling.

We often go through a period of emptiness and mourning, as if our life is over, before we become fully established in the awakened state. It can take a while before the Self is completely born. Meanwhile, the experience is often one of feeling lost, directionless, empty, sad, and unmotivated. This isn't what we expected self-realization to be like! We didn't think that giving up all notions of ourselves would feel like this. We thought everything would finally be easy and clear. Most of all, we thought awakening would result in something stable, an endpoint, a completion, an arrival, not further unfolding.

This feeling of being lost and without motivation is actually the remaining ego's experience of awakeness. The ego felt the same way when it touched into the Self before awakening, which is why it ran from the Self then. But now it can't escape the reality: It's no longer in charge. Its goals are no longer primary; they no longer are the driving or shaping force in life. Something else is shaping life. Something else has taken the helm, and it doesn't operate through the mind as the ego did. A new way of being in the world has to be learned, as the egoic mind is no longer the guiding force.

It takes time before this new way of being feels comfortable and is trusted, but going back to the egoic mind is generally not felt to be an option, although that does happen. Plenty of people awaken and then allow the egoic mind to continue to run the show, as if they had never awakened. In these cases, the person doesn't feel much different after awakening than before, and that can be very confusing. Depending on the amount of conditioning and woundedness that remain, the ego can still be fairly compelling, especially in those aspects of life that need healing.

Whatever conditioning remains to be healed will come up after awakening because it is a time for conditioning to be seen and released. The stirring up of conditioning is disconcerting to those who assume that awakening means the end of conditioning and ego-identification. For most people, awakening isn't the end of all conditioning (just some of it), but awakening makes it much easier to see and heal the conditioning that remains and not continue to identify with it, which only strengthens it.

The potential for conditioning (and the egoic mind) to weaken and drop away increases tremendously after awakening because being aligned with the Self allows conditioning to be seen, accepted, understood, and healed rather than identified with. Mistaken beliefs that fuel conditioned behavior and negative feelings can more easily be uncovered. And in that discovery, the conditioning is healed. As a result, evolution can progress very rapidly after awakening. So if this is your experience, please understand that it's the right experience and what needs to be cleared away is being cleared away so that you can live more truly as the Self.

It often takes at least a couple of years, and often much longer, to become more stabilized in the Self after an awakening. During that time, there's usually an unraveling of conditioning, as just mentioned. For many, the period after awakening may also be a time of modifying the structures in their lives to fit the Self instead of the ego. Anything that is no longer aligned with the Self's intentions is likely to feel unpleasant and uncomfortable, and the person is likely to be moved to change it. Many make enormous changes after awakening and others make none; it depends on how aligned with the Self your life before awakening was. If it was structured around your conditioning and the ego's values, then it will have to change. This is one reason some go back to the egoic mind even after awakening: It is an attempt to maintain the structures that no longer work. The person will probably only be able to do stay ego-identified for so long. It is difficult to have seen the truth and then walk away from where it's calling you.

HOW TO MOVE IN THE WORLD

Awakening is just the beginning of a new journey of the newly born Self in the world. After awakening, the world is still there; wood still needs to be chopped and water carried. Here you are in the world. You didn't ascend into heaven to live happily ever after. Now what?

Learning how to move in the world is the first work of this new Self. What drives our actions now, if not conditioning? It takes a while before we learn to walk on our new baby Buddha legs. Our legs don't move on the same basis anymore. They move on the basis of inner urges, not conditioned ones. The impetus to move and do comes from within, as it always has, only now it is unimpeded by conditioned ideas about what we should and shouldn't do, which have often superseded the Self's inner impetus.

Before awakening, the Self was living through us, but it allowed the ego to direct our actions and behavior. After awakening, the Self becomes the primary director, with the ego taking over occasionally, when remaining conditioning is triggered. The center of our being eventually becomes the Self instead of the ego, and that is a very big shift, and one that will take some time to get used to.

During this transition period, before the Self becomes fully embodied, the ego is still somewhat in play. As a result, this can be a confusing time because we may not feel very different than before awakening. Remaining conditioning still has some power to pull us back into the egoic state of consciousness, although the contraction of consciousness is more fluid than before and less likely to feel like a problem. Now that we know who we are, a trip into the egoic state of consciousness isn't really a problem. We know it's just a trip and not a permanent condition. Before awakening, we resisted feeling contracted. Now we are free to bring more curiosity to what is behind every contraction because we know we are just visiting the ego's world.

This curiosity and willingness to look at conditioning is what allows conditioning to be healed and released. When mistaken beliefs are met repeatedly with curiosity and love and the willingness to see the truth about them, they stop clamoring for our attention and eventually give way. Once the truth about our beliefs is seen, they no longer have the power to grab our attention. We stop paying attention to them because we see that they aren't true. They may still arise, but we don't react to them.

Although our conditioned beliefs may have some truth to them, they are usually more limiting than helpful because they are often not true now, in *this* moment. To find out what's true in the moment, we have to look somewhere other than the egoic mind. Take, for example, the belief that you won't be successful unless you work hard. Few are likely to disagree with that belief. However, is that belief a good guide for your behavior every time it arises in your mind? A thought like that one often arises when we are relaxing, so does that mean we should never relax? Isn't it equally true that relaxing can be beneficial? So what will guide our behavior, if not our conditioned beliefs?

There's something that has been guiding our behavior all along, and our beliefs have either agreed with this something or gotten in its way. This something is the Self. More often, our beliefs both support *and* get in the way of the Self's intentions because we hold many contradictory beliefs. So if beliefs are our guide for what to do, we are bound to feel confused most of the time.

Meanwhile, amidst this confusion, we continue to do whatever we do. Who or what is choosing this action or that one? Are your actions always based on your beliefs about how to act? Or do you sometimes do something completely different? How often have you decided to do something based on a list of pros and cons, only to do the opposite? Who made *that* choice?

In spite of ourselves, life happens, doing happens: Suddenly, we pick up the phone and call someone. Suddenly, we jump out of bed. Suddenly, we stop doing whatever we are doing to do something else. If you pay attention, you see that much of what you do in a day just happens: You just act without thinking about it. Action of this nature is marked by non-resistance, ease, spontaneity, excitement, rightness, and satisfaction. What if all your actions were like that, unencumbered by the usual mental gymnastics?

After awakening, we move through life this way, instead of on the basis of ideas, beliefs, and opinions about what we should and shouldn't do or what is best. We don't assume we know what's best; we just do what the moment calls for. We see that the answer to what to do lies in the moment. This doesn't mean our actions aren't informed by wisdom, but the wisdom that informs them doesn't belong to the mind.

Actions motivated by the Self spring out of nowhere, and those actions will be different from one moment to the next. One moment's actions can't predict another moment's actions. Who knows what the next moment will require? We don't know until it arrives. After awakening, the only formula for life is responding to what is moving now... and now... and now. To the egoic mind, this way of moving through life doesn't make sense, and the egoic mind doesn't like it because it leaves it with nothing to do. However, in truth, that is what's been happening all along, and the egoic mind has only gotten in the way.

WHO YOU REALLY ARE

The illusion of being an individual, a *me*, is so strong that, unless we have had some experience of what is beyond the *me*, no amount of explanation is likely to convince us that we are not who we think we are. The ego is a very realistic illusion. However, once we are on the spiritual path and responding to the longing to discover who we are, the Self begins to insert itself into our life more obviously. Before that, seeing the Truth is only likely to result in fear or confusion. However, once we begin looking for the Truth, it reveals itself.

The truth about who you are is that you are everything. There is only one Being, and that Being is you! This truth is too big for the mind to comprehend. It needs to be seen with something other than the mind. It needs to be experienced.

Even when the Truth is known through experience, it can't be conveyed adequately to those who haven't experienced it. Therefore, what some must take on faith, others know for certainty. The desire to know the Truth, however, prepares the way for the experience of it. That desire, that longing for the Truth, is characteristic of spiritual seekers and felt when the time comes to discover it.

Where does that desire, that longing, come from? It isn't something that *you*, the ego, can make happen. This longing arises out of nowhere and heralds a phase of seeking and discovery. *You* can't desire to know the Truth. Instead, this desire consumes *you* at a certain point, and *you* are its victim. The desire comes from the Self when the Self is ready to incarnate, and *you* must be sacrificed for this to happen.

THE EGO'S NEW ROLE

The ego doesn't ever actually die. After awakening, it continues to function and may still dominate at times, but it is relegated to a subordinate role. The ego, the sense of being a separate individual, is still needed because we continue to function in the world of illusion with others who believe the illusion. In order to get by in this world, where language concurs with the illusion, it's necessary to join in, speak the language, and behave like a separate individual. If we don't, others are likely to lock us up.

After awakening, however, we hold the idea of ourselves more lightly. We know that the *me* isn't the whole story, but for the sake of getting along in the world, we play our part, like an actor who knows that he or she is playing a role. Before awakening, we were only occasionally aware of playing a part. We took ourselves to be real, to be the character we are playing, and now we don't. However, as long as others take us to be real, then to interact with them, we need to play the part of this character. Only now, we know we are just pretending.

Playing this part isn't difficult because the ego and the personality are still present. However, now the ego will do the Self's bidding, and that's a big difference. Before awakening, *my will* was the driving force; now *Thy will* drives the life. The ego is more like a puppet now, like a costume or vehicle for the Self, instead of an independent entity.

The Self begins to live through us after awakening. Some of our conditioning is still adhered to because some conditioning is necessary for managing physical reality. However, conditioning that's limiting and interferes with the Self's embodiment in the world is likely to fall away, although that may take years and may never be complete. How completely our conditioning falls away depends on its strength and how much awareness and acceptance we bring to our ideas and beliefs when they arise—and Grace.

After awakening, the Self and the ego join together to accomplish the Self's goals on earth, which couldn't be fully accomplished when the ego was in control. Consequently our life often changes dramatically after awakening. Before, we pursued a set of goals related to conditioning and the ego's desires. Now, we move to a different drummer, one that has little concern for customs, conventions, and other conditioned ways of being unless they serve the Self's purposes.

After awakening, we are likely to be experienced by others as independent, different, unconventional, and freethinking because we don't follow the dictates of much of our conditioning. This doesn't mean we won't follow the rules, when breaking the rules would only cause unnecessary problems; but if breaking the rules or rocking the boat serves a purpose in opening people's eyes to an injustice or some other cause the Self feels committed to, we probably won't hesitate to break the rules or rock the boat.

Above all, after awakening, we are true to the Self, which is literally moving through us. Before awakening, the Self's nudges, which came through as intuition, drives, and dreams, were easy to miss or ignore. But after awakening, ignoring these promptings becomes much more difficult. And because the mind is no longer so noisy and cluttered by conditioning after awakening, on occasion, the Self can be heard in the mind in the form of a word or phrase. After awakening, the Self's voice and intuitions are more prominent and apparent, and the usual thoughts aren't present to argue with these messages. So messages get through loud and clear, and action just happens.

FEAR'S ROLE IN THE ILLUSION

Before awakening, the voice that speaks the loudest is the ego's, which operates from fear. The sense of being a separate entity is the cause of fear. That feeling of separation impels the ego to organize around protecting itself from what it feels separate from, whether that be other people, animals, objects, or ideas it finds threatening.

The ego enlists the mind and the body to protect its interests. Whatever gives the ego an advantage in relation to others is seen by the ego as necessary for survival. The ego's definition of what it needs for survival is very broad and extends far beyond what we usually think of as necessary for survival.

The fear of not surviving is the most basic fear; all others boil down to that one. The fear of falling, being harmed, failing, loss, and even not being loved are all part of the fear of not surviving. As human animals, we have a basic instinct to survive, and fear is the force that drives that instinct. It mobilizes our energy to act on behalf of the *me*. The mind continually analyzes our actions and their results according to how they affect *me* and, more specifically, the survival of *me* and its ability to survive well.

Fear and the sense of being a *me* are irredeemably intertwined, until we realize there is no *me*, only the Self. Once that realization happens, fear is no longer predominant, although it still operates instinctually when it's needed, to protect against real danger.

Before awakening, fear is the strongest motivating force, although it masquerades itself quite well. We aren't generally aware of the extent of our fear because it motivates our behavior unconsciously. Even something as simple as making a friend is at least partly motivated by fear, since our connections with others help us survive. In the egoic state of consciousness, nearly every action has a selfish motive, and what underlies that self-interest is the fear of not surviving.

What's in it for the *me* doesn't have to be obvious rewards, such as money or fame. Something as simple as feeling good about *me* will do. We often do things just to feel good about ourselves because doing them increases the likelihood of our survival. Most of our altruistic actions are not selfless at all, but serve the motive of winning the love and admiration of others, which increases our standing in the world and therefore our ability to survive.

This doesn't mean that spontaneous charity never happens in the egoic state of consciousness, but it happens despite it. Even when we are deeply embedded in the egoic state of consciousness, we may perform an altruistic deed because the Self breaks through and acts spontaneously to fulfill a need. As we evolve, the Self breaks through increasingly, and ego-based action becomes less frequent.

Even after awakening, we can fall prey to ego-inflation after doing something altruistic. Although the ego may not be involved in an altruistic act, it often shows up afterwards as pride, and tries to get something for itself in the form of admiration, praise, or a more tangible reward. Even those who manifest the Self easily and freely in the world still find their egos trying to reestablish themselves from time to time, until they don't anymore.

Even after awakening, the *me* thought is the most persistent thought. Nearly every thought that appears in the mind begins with "I": "I am...." "I like...." "I want...." "I think...." "I will...." "I have...." "I wish...." "I was...." "I feel...." However, our relationship to that thought changes after self-realization. Before awakening, who we are seems like the *me* and everything it thinks about itself. After awakening, we see that we are not the *me*, but the awareness of the *me*. We are no longer identified with the *me*, but with what is aware of the *me*. Later, we come to see that who we are is not only the awareness of everything, but who we are is also everything.

The egoic state of consciousness is identification with the *me*. It is the belief that we are the *me*. When we wake up, we awaken from the illusion of *me*, and we see that we are the Oneness that is everything and that we just pretended for a while to be *me*.

Even if you have little awareness of your true nature, you wouldn't be reading this if you weren't ready to experience it more fully. Experiencing it is more simple and ordinary than you may think, and everyone has had many brief glimpses of it. You may have had an experience of it in your dreams and still have a faint memory of that. The experience of it is often first introduced to people through their dreams, as a way of fanning the flames of spiritual longing.

The longing is what brings us home to the Self. That longing is the inner call we follow to get there. The longing is based on an unconscious memory of Home. When the time comes, the Self calls us Home.

At first, the *me* answers the call because it believes there is something in it for it, particularly spiritual power, which it assumes will help it attain its goals. Spiritual seekers often get started on the path because they think that spiritual practices and what they discover on the spiritual path will get them what they want. At this level, spiritual seekers are no different than materialists, who believe that money or worldly power will get them what they want. The actions of these spiritual seekers are still motivated by the desire to get something for themselves, for the *me.*

Eventually, the spiritual seeker matures, the longing increases, the seeker encounters teachers who call into question the seeker's motives, and then fulfilling the longing itself becomes the reason for being on the path.

When the longing becomes a burning, it consumes the *me.* Who we think we are can't withstand the fire of Truth because it consumes everything that isn't real. The *me* can't survive because it never existed in the first place. It was just something we pretended to be. The Real is so juicy and alive that, once we experience it, we can never settle for the false again. The remembrance of the Real drives us on the path until we become merged with it.

We think the *me* is necessary, until we see that it isn't. This realization only happens once the Self has taken on some embodiment and we see that life goes on happily and smoothly without reliance on the *me.* Before that, trusting that the *me* isn't necessary is difficult. In truth, life goes on much more happily and smoothly with the *me* out of the driver's seat. The *me* has never been necessary. Nothing else has really ever been living life but the Real. The *me* is a counterfeit that stepped in and tried to live our life, but it never succeeded. It only succeeded in causing confusion, uncertainty, discontentment, doubt, shame, guilt, and fear.

The *me's* job is to create these negative feelings because, without them, there would be no *me.* Without a sense of separation, which defines the ego, those feelings wouldn't exist. Separation results particularly in fear, but also in confusion, uncertainty, discontentment, doubt, shame, and guilt because of the ego's lack of connection with its source, the Self. The ego's job, then, is to manipulate the environment to eliminate, or at least diminish, fear and the other uncomfortable feelings that accompany separation. The ego creates the problem, or we could say that it *is* the problem, and then it invests itself in solving it.

The ego creates strategies for achieving its desires. It believes that if it can get certain desires met, it will be free of fear and the sense of separation. Only after many desires have been met and the ego still isn't happy, does the ego become open to the possibility that happiness lies in the Oneness that is spoken of in spiritual teachings instead of in the pursuit of other desires, which have only led to further suffering. Only after failing time and time again to attain happiness does the ego turn to the spiritual path to try to achieve its goals.

THE EGOIC MIND'S REJECTION OF ONENESS

The ego doesn't realize that the pursuit of Oneness will lead to its dissolution until that possibility arises. It becomes very uncomfortable when the Real appears on the scene. Fear often arises very strongly, accompanied by a barrage of reasons to discount the Real, particularly the realness of the Real. The egoic mind simply can't comprehend the Real and, as a result, declares it false.

Fortunately, the ego is not the only thing having the experience of the Real, because that would be the end of the story. We would turn away, and that would be that. However, that which is experiencing the Real is the Real itself, as well as itself masquerading as the ego. And when the time comes for us to embody the Self, the ego will have to step aside, although the ego won't do that without a fight.

When the Self is experienced, the egoic mind comes up with reasons for turning away from the Self and remaining in the illusion. The experience of the Self is one of no-thing-ness, emptiness, and clear space, which indeed seems like nothing to the ego. When the Self is finally experienced, the ego concludes that there is nothing there, and the ego goes back to thing-ness, which it finds more interesting.

No-thing-ness is not interesting to the mind. There is nothing in no-thing-ness for the mind or the ego. The mind's job is to compare, contrast, evaluate, and discriminate between things; so of course it isn't interested in no-thing-ness. The Self lives in a dimension other than the mind, and the mind can't go there. It doesn't have words to describe that dimension, and no words could fully encompass it.

The Self can't be experienced through the usual senses. However, the ego is convinced that the senses provide an accurate picture of reality, and that's the problem. The ego thinks that physical reality is the only thing that is real and that whatever it can't sense isn't real. From the Self's standpoint, the truth is quite different: Physical reality is only part of what is real, and what is most real can't be experienced by the five senses. The challenge of awakening is breaking through the illusion.

Ironically, the mind is required to see through the illusion. The very thing that presents such a stumbling block to seeing the Truth is what is needed to see through the illusion. It's accomplished by using the mind to see the false within it. When the mind is being used this way, it is by the Self. The ego doesn't have the capacity to use the mind this way. At a certain point the Self inserts itself into the mind and, like a wise teacher, shows the student what is false about the mind.

This is a very big step in evolution because, before that, there's often little awareness of what the egoic mind is thinking, only unconscious reactions to it. Now the mind is turned in on itself to discover the validity of its thoughts. This is when the egoic mind begins to unravel because so little is found to be true.

All sorts of untrue ideas and assumptions exist in the egoic mind, including many opposite and contradictory ones. The egoic mind reasons one way on one day and another way on the next. It concludes one thing, and then it concludes the opposite. It wants one thing, and then it wants something different. It is fickle because its conclusions are based on contradictory evidence and beliefs. The egoic mind's beliefs, ideas, and opinions aren't coherent and consistent; so how could its conclusions be? Here is an exercise that will help you free yourself from the egoic mind:

Exercise: Breaking the Tyranny of the Mind

This inquiry will help you see the inconsistencies of the egoic mind, and that discovery can help free you from it.

What is one of your beliefs or opinions? Is it true? What about the opposite belief or opinion? Is that true too sometimes? Is it even possible to have a true belief? Our beliefs have some truth to them, but how much? Most beliefs are partial truths, and many have very little truth to them.

Continue to examine other beliefs and opinions you hold, especially the ones you hold most strongly. What ideas, beliefs, or opinions arise most often in your mind? What beliefs do you hold most strongly? Is there a theme to them? Where did you get them? Are they true?

Despite its unreliability, the egoic mind is sure of its viewpoint, and it can be very convincing. A thought arises, and often a sense of great certainty is attached to it, so we agree with it without examining it. Our thoughts can be very convincing, regardless of whether they are true or not. Having an egoic mind is like having a propaganda machine in our head, but who is spewing propaganda and why?

There's no answer to who is spewing this propaganda because there's no one "behind the curtain." Like the wizard of Oz, the ego isn't what we think it is. The ego has no real substance; it's nothing more than a bunch of disparate beliefs and ideas. Behind the ego, there is no one who has all the answers. The ego is more like a computer that has been programmed with platitudes and beliefs. Like the mechanical gypsies found at carnivals, you put your money in, and out pops an answer: You never know what will pop into your mind, but you can be sure *something* will if you give it your attention (your money).

Why the egoic mind acts like a propaganda machine is simple, really: It is the mechanism that keeps the illusion going. The mind is programmed to make the illusion believable. The egoic mind is part of the Self's game of hide and seek. Who programmed it? The Self, of course (there is no one else), but the specific programming it contains depends on our genetics and environment. Our egoic mind is programmed to create the particular experiences the Self intends to have through us until we awaken from the illusion and the Self becomes embodied. After that, the programming only serves when necessary.

It turns out that the egoic mind is part of the human animal and a tool for both the human and the Self, but it isn't what it pretends to be: who we are. The egoic mind dictates the supposed truth to us about who we are and how things are, and we believe it, until we don't. The egoic mind is an imposter dictator: It tells us this and it tells us that, but it is spinning a false reality.

Beyond the mind lies Awareness, which is aware of the mind, the body, and everything that exists, and that is who we are. We are the Awareness that allows the egoic mind to spin its illusions and create the drama in which the Awareness, the Self, delights. There's no mistake here. The illusory ego and the programming associated with it are all intended to make manifest the Self's playground. Meanwhile, the Self participates in its creation by being aware of it all.

Chapter 3
Seeing Through the Illusion

THE VOICE OF THE EGO

Being able to see through the illusion of the false self and dis-identify from it and the false reality it creates is largely a matter of getting to know the ego (via the voice in your head), really seeing what it's like and what it's up to. Once you see the truth about the ego, ignoring the egoic mind's chatter becomes much easier. And once you are able to ignore the egoic mind, you land in reality, the present moment, where it is possible to experience and express your true nature.

The ego presents itself in the mind in two ways:

1. Much of the time, the ego is the voice of "I": "I like...," "I want...," "I need...," "I will...," "I am...," "I was...," "I can't...," I wish...," "I feel...," "I hate...," and so on.

2. The ego also presents itself as an outside voice. It talks to you as if it were another person: "You should...," "You are...," You can't...," "You won't...," "You need...," "People shouldn't...," Life is...," "They are...," "He shouldn't...," and so on.

The ego takes on a number of different personas, or guises, when it speaks to us mentally as a voice outside ourselves. One of the most common guises is The Judge. This is the voice that judges you, others, and situations. It can be sharp and unkind. The ego also often takes on an authoritarian voice, which we could call The Tyrant: It tells you what to do and when and how to do it. It hurries and pushes you and sometimes demeans you. Then there is The Martyr: The ego often takes on this guise after feeling victimized by The Tyrant, by someone else, or by life. At other times, the ego pretends to be a spiritual guide, which we could call The Guru. When the ego is acting in that capacity, it takes on a wise tone and advises you on spiritual matters, but The Guru has no real wisdom, only a lot of misunderstandings and judgments. Another favorite guise is that of a friend: The Buddy. In that guise, the ego chats with you like a friend would, but The Buddy is a friend that you don't need. And then there's The Pleasure-Seeker, which goads you into overindulging in physical pleasures. It's responsible for overeating and other addictions, which are really compensations for dealing with the stress created by The Judge, The Tyrant, and other negative personas. Look and see for yourself what other guises your ego might take on:

Exercise: Discovering the Voices of Your Ego

Discovering the various voices of your ego may take several days of observation. It might be helpful to jot down names for the various personas when you discover them so that you can see the variety that is there.

Notice the tone of the voice in your head. The tone gives you a clue to what persona the ego is taking on. Is the tone kind and accepting? If so, the ego might be showing up as The Buddy or The Mother. Is the tone mean? That could be the ego as The Judge, The Tormentor, The Tyrant, or The Bad Mother. Is the voice offering advice? That could be the ego as The Good Mother, The Guru, or The Teacher.

What is the voice in your head like most of the time? Is it kind and accepting, or is it unkind and not accepting? Is it happy or unhappy? Is it friendly and chatty, or is it bossy and judgmental? Is it optimistic or pessimistic? Is it angry? Fearful? Negative? Grandiose? Complaining? Arrogant? Self-pitying? Self-righteous? Self-deprecating? Which voices grab your attention the most? Which do you give voice to, or identify with, most easily?

Everyone's ego is different, and everyone's ego takes on different guises, although some guises are universal, like the ones just named. Some of the more universal guises will be explored more fully later in this chapter, but there are many others. Some egos wear fairly positive guises much of the time, while other egos can be extremely negative. Whether the voice in your head shows up positively or negatively, the voice is still the ego, and the ego isn't wise enough to run our lives, even though it tries to convince us otherwise. The ego's negative guises are designed to scare us into listening to it or to create other uncomfortable feelings that keep us involved with it. And the positive guises are an attempt to sweet-talk us into listening to it. But the egoic mind is still not worth listening to. When we stop giving our attention to the voice in our head, we discover another way to be and move in the world.

THE MOST CONVINCING THOUGHT

The illusion of the false self, the ego, is created and maintained by the most convincing thought of all: "I." When we think "I...," we really believe that is what we believe. For example, when we think "I like hot weather" or "I want a new car," we really believe this preference or desire is true for us. It defines, or identifies, us: "I'm someone who likes hot weather." "I'm someone who wants a new car." Or if we think "I feel lost," we really believe that is true about us—and meaningful. We don't see that it is just a thought, which if believed, becomes true, a self-fulfilling prophecy. It seems true because we believe it, but it is not intrinsically true. It's just a thought, after all.

Where do thoughts come from? Thoughts arise out of nowhere. Just because a thought is happening in your own head doesn't mean it is any more true than a thought that arises in someone else's head. However, we become attached to our thoughts. We identify with them as how *I* feel or what *I* like. But who is this *I*?

Is it true that you are who your thoughts describe? Your thoughts describe you and give you a sense of being a certain way, but who are they describing? Aren't they just describing a character you identify as you, who likes certain things, has certain dreams and desires, believes certain things, sees himself or herself and life a certain way? Is that who you really are, or is that the character you are playing? Who is it that is aware of the thoughts that define you? Who is it that is actually reading this and moving your body, breathing, seeing, touching, smelling, and experiencing life? Does the character do this, or is there something else here that is character-less, that is just purely experiencing life, without ideas about liking or disliking, wanting or not wanting?

Thoughts about *I* create a character. When we believe these thoughts (which are very, very convincing), we begin to feel and think and act like that character. This is the false, or conditioned, self, and it's derived largely from thoughts about *I*. The stronger you believe your thoughts about *I*, the more powerful the illusion of self, the false self, is.

Exercise: Discovering the Character You Are Playing

Get a pencil and paper, and jot down a description of the character that your mind describes as you. What characteristics and qualities belong to that character? What does that character look like? How does that character behave? How does it feel much of the time? What are its beliefs? How does it see itself in relationship to others and to the world? This is the character you are playing, but it isn't who you really are.

As we evolve, we learn to take this character more lightly, we joke about it; we can even enjoy it. And eventually, we all wake up out of it. We come to see that it was created by believing our thoughts about ourselves. Meanwhile, the Being that we really are has been present in this life, living, breathing, moving, speaking, and acting through our body-mind. This Being, the Self, lets us pretend that we are the character we think we are; however, this Being is not the character, but the consciousness behind this life and, ultimately, behind all life.

Yes, the "I" thought is extremely convincing. If it weren't, the illusion of being someone couldn't be maintained. Eventually, the *I* is seen as being an illusion, and life and the character continue, but with more joy and ease, and with love for this character and all other characters because it sees the truth: We are all made of the same Consciousness, and we're only playing at being different. What fun!

THE "I" THOUGHT IS USELESSS

Have you ever noticed how useless your thoughts about yourself are? Most thoughts about ourselves are an attempt to define ourselves as this or that: "I like this, not that"; "I want this, not that"; "I feel this, not that"; "I believe this, not that"; "I am this, not that." However, thoughts about ourselves define ourselves only temporarily, since thoughts about ourselves don't stay the same: Sometimes we like or want or feel or believe something, and sometimes we like or want or feel or believe something else. We create our sense of self through thoughts about ourselves, but the sense of self is always changing. It isn't stable or consistent. Moreover, it's made up: One day, we define and imagine ourselves one way, and another day, we define and imagine ourselves another way.

Do we need thoughts about ourselves to exist or to function? We obviously don't need them to exist because we still exist even when we aren't thinking about ourselves and when we are asleep. Do we need thoughts about ourselves to function? It's a little trickier to see that we don't need thoughts about ourselves or thoughts in general to function. But if you look closely at this, you discover that many actions are spontaneous and do not stem from a thought first. In fact, a lot of thoughts are thoughts about actions that have already taken place (the past) and thoughts about actions that have yet to take place or may never take place (the future), none of which are relevant to the present moment. Other thoughts are primarily thoughts that accompany our actions, that evaluate what we're doing, remind us of what to do next, complain about it, argue about how to do it, and any number of other thoughts.

Do we need any of these thoughts to accomplish what needs to be done? Our thoughts often make us less efficient because when we are absorbed in thought, we are less present to what we are doing. And our thoughts about what we're doing often hinder or complicate what we're doing instead of making it easier. They may cause us to doubt ourselves as we're doing something or question why we are doing it or give us pros and cons for doing it, all of which can confuse us. When you really begin to notice what's going on, you see that thoughts about yourself and thoughts about what you are doing, including what you should or shouldn't do and when and how, are not necessary and are, in fact, often problematic.

Exercise: Discovering the Uselessness of Thoughts

As you move about your day, notice the thoughts that arise about yourself and what you are doing.

Do you really need thoughts that tell you how or when to do something, or that evaluate what you are doing? Don't you already know, for instance, to lock the door, without the mind reminding you? Or when you are locking the door or doing something else, do you need any opinions, judgments, memories, fantasies, or desires that are showing up in the mind at that time? Do those thoughts help you function better? Do they help you in any other way? Or do they just distract you from being present to whatever you are doing and whatever is showing up in life? Can you find a useful thought, one you really need?

Thoughts about yourself create the false self, and you don't need the false self to function, although you are programmed to believe you *are* the false self and that your thoughts about yourself and your life are necessary to function. You are programmed to believe a lie! What an amazing thing that is! That is why this world is called an illusion by those who see through the illusion. The illusion is that you are the egoic self and your thoughts are true and helpful. The Illusion leads you to believe that the false self is what is living your life, when in fact, what is living your life is responsible for creating everything, including the illusion that you are who you *think* you are. The key to seeing through the illusion is noticing your thoughts and how inconsistent, untrue, useless, and primarily negative, they actually are. You use the capacity to be aware of your thoughts to free yourself from the illusion that your thoughts are true.

Seeing that thinking about yourself doesn't serve is a crucial step in seeing through the illusion because that's all the false self is: thoughts about itself. Once you start ignoring your thoughts about yourself, that is, once you stop being involved with thinking about yourself, you discover that you have never needed those thoughts and that they have only taken you away from what is true and real. They have taken you away from the experience of your real Self living in the present moment and away from moving spontaneously and naturally through life. You have never needed any of those thoughts about yourself. You have always been living life in spite of them. Who you really are has allowed you to believe the illusion, while it has continued to be alive through you and move you in its own way through life.

THE EGOIC MIND IS LIKE A RADIO STATION

If you pay attention to the mind, you will see how similar it is to what is played on a radio station. Often the mind will just comment, or report, on things: "The sky is so blue. We haven't had rain in a long time. The leaves are beginning to change colors." These are often the kinds of things we say to others too. We voice our observations. We speak the obvious. When the mind puts observations into words, it's just making conversation, and so are people when they make such observations. These observations aren't necessary for life to function, although there's nothing wrong with them. When the egoic mind is simply observing, that's when it is most benign. Then the egoic mind is like the news report: "It will be in the upper eighties today with scattered thunderstorms." "The Senate is going to vote on the bill today." "He was convicted and sent to jail for life." No spin, just the facts.

The egoic mind also offers advice, just like the radio: "Don't overcook the noodles or they'll get mushy." It offers advice when you might need it based on information it has stored on a variety of subjects. How helpful. Or is it? We assume we need this information, these reminders. But do we really? We must already know that tip about cooking noodles or our mind wouldn't be able to tell us that. The helpfulness of the voice in our head is highly overrated.

One of the most obvious ways the egoic mind is like a radio station, especially like talk radio, is that the mind has an opinion about everything, whether you are informed about that subject or not. This phenomenon is particularly obvious in talk radio: The moderators and guests have strong opinions, whether they are informed or not. They are often simply giving voice to their egoic minds and believing them, and hoping others will believe them too. The ego's way of convincing others of its opinion is to state the opinion firmly and loudly, not necessarily to support it with facts. Yes, the egoic mind is like a radio station, and radio stations are like the egoic mind.

The egoic mind, like the radio and TV, loves to gossip and to tell sensational and shocking stories, and tales of criminal and taboo-breaking behavior. Our egoic minds feed and become stronger on the same stuff soap operas thrive on, so that's another way our minds are like radio or TV programs (and vice versa). Our egos love anything that stirs up our emotions; and bad news, celebrity gossip, and scary stories give the ego more to be stirred up about, just in case it's not coming up with enough on its own. And, like a radio or TV program, our minds grab our attention and are hard to turn off, especially when what is being said activates our emotions.

One very important way the egoic mind is different from a radio program is that it speaks to us personally. It's like having someone standing over your shoulder, watching your every move, offering you information, correcting you, making you worry or doubt or question, evaluating you, and telling you what to do. If a friend behaved toward you like the egoic mind does, he or she probably wouldn't be your friend for long! We not only put up with the egoic mind, but we also *believe* it; we trust it. We think it is who we are.

The radio doesn't talk to you directly like your egoic mind does. But like the radio, the voice in your head comes out of nowhere and intrudes into your activities, only in a more personal way, which makes the voice in your head more compelling than the radio, less easy to tune out. When someone is personally addressing you, you listen!

The questions we need to ask ourselves are: Do we want to be feeding the egoic mind by listening to it? Is that really where we want to put our attention? Is that voice saying anything useful, anything helpful? The egoic mind takes us in some pretty dissatisfying directions if we let it. It can consume a lot of our time and energy. Having opinions and emotions is exhausting and doesn't feel good. We are left feeling contracted, stressed, and drained.

No, the egoic mind doesn't have much to offer when you really take a look at it. It's a lousy station to tune into, not nearly as helpful as PBS! The good news is we can learn to tune out the egoic mind and see the voice in our head as something like a radio station: impersonal and not belonging to us. We can learn to not engage with it.

What is it that is capable of not engaging with the egoic mind? That is who you really are. The egoic mind may talk to you personally and seem like your own voice, but it isn't. That is the illusion. You aren't your mind. What a relief! Then you can begin to see that life is carried on just fine without all the egoic mind's "help." And life will go much better, and you will be much happier.

In service to busting the ego's game, let's examine more closely some of the guises it takes on:

THE EGO AS THE TYRANT

The ego often plays the role of the tyrant: It prods and pushes, bosses, and evaluates. The Tyrant's voice can be harsh, demanding, demeaning, and unkind. It can also be rational, reasonable, parental, and authoritative. Either way, we tend to believe that voice and follow it. When we are identified with the ego, The Tyrant plays a big role in guiding us through our day and, we think, making sure we get things done, and get them done right. We are convinced that we need The Tyrant to keep up with life, without realizing that The Tyrant is the one that generates the to-do list that keeps us so busy.

The ego, as The Tyrant, not only tells us what to do, but also when and how to do it. It devises a list of things to do and checks to see how the list is going: "Did you do that? How well did you do that? What do you have left to do? Can you do it? Will you get it done in time? Will it be done well enough? Will you run into trouble? What problems might arise? How will you deal with those problems?"

The Tyrant is a compelling voice because we really believe we need it to function. We really believe we wouldn't get anything done if we didn't listen to it. We're so used to that voice that we don't even question what it is telling us or whether we even need it. Where do its instructions and ideas come from? Is it wise? Is it true?

The Tyrant is developed through the training we receive from authority figures, particularly parents. It's a composite of the authority figures we have known, which we have internalized, and of other things we've learned. So now, as adults, instead of parents and teachers telling us what to do and when and how to do it, The Tyrant plays the role of a parent, teacher, or boss. This is a natural psychological process. The trouble is that, just as parents don't always know what is best for us, The Tyrant doesn't either. It doesn't have the wisdom to guide us; it's just mouthing what we've learned.

We actually don't need to have our conditioning voiced like that, since we automatically respond to life according to our conditioning. The voice is redundant and unnecessary. Like the ego, this aspect of the ego is a sham. It's an imposter. It isn't who we are, and it isn't wise; it only pretends to be.

That The Tyrant is unnecessary becomes obvious when you drop out of the ego and begin to live from the Self. When you live from the Self, you draw on your conditioning when necessary: You still don't cross busy streets without looking or touch hot stoves. You don't need The Tyrant to remind you of these things.

Once you realize you don't need the Tyrant, you can ignore its voice, and when you ignore it long enough, it eventually falls away. What a miracle! No more voice telling you what to do and how to do it, and evaluating your every move. No more going over lists and checking them twice! When we stop listening to The Tyrant, this aspect of the ego eventually gives up and disappears, although usually not overnight.

The real problem with The Tyrant is that it causes stress. Instead of being helpful, listening to its voice takes the joy out of life and keeps our attention focused unnecessarily in the mental realm and therefore outside the present moment, where true happiness and true guidance are available. It makes us less present to life. And when we are less present to life, we are less effective and efficient and less happy and at peace with life. The Tyrant actually interferes with functioning optimally and with enjoying whatever we're doing. Its voice is not just annoying. It's much worse than that: It causes us to worry and hurry and feel insufficient. It gives us the sense that there's never enough time and that we're never done with our to-do list. This is not a state that is conducive to peace, love, and contentment, but just the opposite.

Fortunately, if you don't listen to The Tyrant, you will be guided by something wiser to do what needs to be done. You also will be guided to do what is of real value, and you will make time for that, for such things as love, creativity, meditation, service, learning, growing, developing your talents, doing what makes your heart sing, and just being. In the ego's world, there's no end to working, striving, and perfecting. But we are also here to enjoy life, to create, and to express our uniqueness, not just accomplish tasks.

Enjoying life doesn't mean doing nothing, but being present to whatever you are doing. Then everything you do becomes infused with joy and peace, and you are able to express love naturally. You have the energy to do what needs to be done because your energy isn't being taken up in doing unnecessary things or in being stressed.

To begin practicing this new way of being, just start noticing the tyrannical voice in your head and recognize it as programming you don't need. Accept that it's there. Don't fight or argue with this voice, because this aspect of the ego is just part of being human. And then, just be present to whatever you are doing, or just be. Life is much simpler, more joyous, less stressful, and runs much more smoothly without the tyranny of the ego.

THE EGO AS THE MARTYR

The Martyr is another familiar voice in the head for many. It often shows up after we have been listening to The Tyrant and have exhausted ourselves by trying to do too much or by trying to be perfect. When we give in to the dictates of The Tyrant, we often feel martyred, and the unhappiness and ego-domination continues, as the ego shifts personas to The Martyr.

The Martyr shows up as the voice of feeling unappreciated, overlooked, overworked, and abused: "Nobody notices all the things I do. Nobody cares. All I do is work, work, work. Life isn't any fun. I sacrifice so much, and what do I get for it? I work so hard, and for what?" The Martyr is the voice of self-pity. Being martyred gives the ego a sense of being special. Being a martyr is an identity, but a very unhappy one. When we are identified with

The Martyr, we feel burdened, sad, worn out, unacknowledged, and not respected.

The Martyr's sad story can result in a lot of complaining. The Complainer and The Martyr are closely related. Both of these personas try to manipulate others and life with their complaints. The unconscious strategy of The Martyr is to make others around The Martyr miserable so that someone will notice and offer some reward, attention, or appreciation.

The best way to avoid The Martyr is to not identify with The Tyrant, which causes us to push ourselves too hard and to lose sight of the joy of being alive. When life becomes only about what we have done and accomplished, we do feel martyred—and we are. We are martyred by The Tyrant, who puts us in that unhappy position. Then The Martyr turns around and persecutes everyone else, which is a very poor strategy for getting what it wants. The ego is not rational, and its strategies not only don't work, but they also backfire.

THE EGO AS THE JUDGE

All judgments come from the ego, and they don't serve us or life well. That is another great illusion: We think our judgments are useful, but they aren't. We are programmed to believe that the judgments that run through our minds are correct, meaningful, and serve a purpose. However, judgments are the ego's ineffective response to life and, more important, a way the ego makes itself feel superior in relationship to others. The sense of rightness and superiority that comes from judging gives the ego a sense of existing, even though the ego doesn't actually exist, except as a mental construct.

The ego is the *sense* of being separate and distinct from others. All the ego really is, is the *feeling* of being a separate individual, a *me*. One of the ways the sense of being *me* is maintained is through judgments, which literally separate us from others. By making ourselves right and others wrong, judgments help maintain a sense of *me* as separate from who or what is being judged.

Another benefit of judging, to the ego, is that the feeling of being right helps the ego feel safe in the world. Believing that its perceptions are right and therefore superior gives the ego a sense of security in this chaotic and unpredictable world. Judging doesn't actually create security, but judging provides the ego with a sense of security. However, the truth is that judging is more likely to undermine our security than ensure it, since judging damages our connection with others, who are important to our survival.

Let's take a moment to examine the experience of judging:

Exercise: Examining How Judgments Make You Feel

Think of a time when you had a judgment about yourself or about someone else. How did that feel? Did it make you feel happy, peaceful, and content with life? (Because that is how you would like to feel, right?) To the ego, judgments feel good because they make the ego feel right and superior. But does feeling right and superior actually feel good? Is that how you would like to feel all the time? Is feeling right and superior worth not feeling happy, peaceful, and content with life? That's the trade-off.

You don't have to feel the way judgments make you feel if you don't give the judgments that come into your mind your attention and if you don't speak them. But before you can ignore these judgments, you might have to be convinced that all that judgments do is hurt you, hurt others, and keep you tied to the egoic state of consciousness. They don't bring about the change in others you think they might but, instead, they damage relationships. Judgments kill love. Are your judgments (which are just thoughts) worth it? If you never voice another judgment in your life, you will be much happier.

Like the "I" thought, the voice in our head that is The Judge is very convincing. Notice the strength, power, and certainty behind your judgments. And notice the contraction you feel when you think them, and especially when you speak them. The Judge takes on a very specific tone of voice and physical stance. When you are identified with The Judge and speaking a judgment, the body is tense and leans forward, and the voice gets louder and sharper. The Judge is tense, harsh, and not particularly just. The Judge doesn't represent the innate wisdom and discrimination of your true nature. To discern what is right for you or wrong for you in any moment, you don't need The Judge.

Instead of being wise, The Judge is essentially a complainer. Judgments express the ego's dissatisfaction with ourselves, with others, and with life. Judgments are easy to come by because the ego is dissatisfied with life most of the time. Dissatisfaction is the ego's primary experience of life, and judgments represent the ego's justification for being unhappy and for not accepting something: "I should have known better; I'm really stupid." "He shouldn't have done that; he's so inconsiderate." "Life shouldn't be so hard; life is terrible." All the ways we, others, and life fall short, in the ego's opinion, are a cause for judgment.

Judgments keep us in resistance to life. They uphold the sense of separation that is the ego, and they keep us in a state of unhappiness. The funny thing is we really believe that judging ourselves, others, and situations has some value in changing what we don't like. But life doesn't change because we judge it, nor do people. Judgments are no way to win people over to our point of view. And yet that is often what we are attempting to do when we judge someone: "If you weren't so lazy, you would get off the couch and help me." We try to manipulate others to comply with our wishes by judging them.

Judgments are unpleasant for everyone, so why indulge The Judge? Once you see what the ego is up to with judgments, you can let the judgments come and go in your mind without touching them. They don't really belong to you, not the real you, anyway. The ego is a pretty nasty creature at times, and The Judge is one of its most destructive guises. The ego in this guise has a demeanor of being helpful, right, and discerning. But The Judge is none of these; it is more of a bully.

THE EGO AS THE GURU

The ego can pretend to be good and wise, but that doesn't make it so. It can sound like it has your best interests at heart, but the ego is a con man. Underneath the supposed wisdom is judgment, because The Guru is essentially The Judge, but on spiritual matters instead of mundane ones. The ego as The Guru is a con man because it cons us into thinking it's guiding us spiritually, when it's really creating the same contraction, discontentment, stress, and striving the ego is known for. When we are aligned with our true nature, we feel relaxed, at peace with life, content, happy, and loving. And we are naturally attuned to the wisdom of the Self. Listening to The Guru, however, doesn't bring such peace and contentment, but only more striving and the sense that we still don't measure up. The Guru shakes its finger at us, saying:

"You'll never be enlightened. You have to be more (fill in the blank) and less (fill in the blank)."

The Guru is often referred to as *the spiritual ego* because it is the ego in spiritual guise, the ego that is trying to be spiritual by following rules and precepts to the letter. The ego doesn't know how to "do" spirituality; it only knows how to mimic it: It pretends to be kind, holy, good, but it doesn't want kindness, holiness, or goodness. It pretends these things only because it wants something else: power, superiority, respect, control, or other things it values. To the ego, spirituality is a means to an end, a means to get more of something or to better one's position in life. The ego thinks that being spiritual will get it what it wants.

The spiritual ego drives people to try to attain enlightenment, when enlightenment is not something anyone can attain, least of all by striving, but quite the opposite. The spiritual ego strives for perfection because that is its idea of spirituality: "Be perfect, don't make any mistakes, know everything, be wise." It hopes to attain such perfection through practices, abstentions, and other means, but these activities are engaged in for the wrong reasons: to strengthen and empower the *me* instead of to dissolve it.

The Guru speaks to us primarily in *shoulds:* "You should meditate twice a day." "You should be present." "You should be nice." "You shouldn't drink so much." "You should get to bed earlier." "You should be doing your life purpose." "You should be saving the world." The word *should* is a sign of the ego. When the Self motivates us to meditate or be kinder or more present, or even to take better care of ourselves, it doesn't inspire us through a thought, but through an inner impetus to do these things. That impetus is true guidance coming from the Self. Such subtle nudges and intuitive messages are continually being sent to us, but we may miss them if we are wrapped up in our thoughts.

It's easy to tell the difference between true guidance coming from the Self and the false guidance of The Guru, besides the fact that the former comes through intuitively and as a drive, and the latter comes through as a thought. True guidance is received without resistance, unless the ego comes in later and resists the impetus or drive to act. The Guru's guidance, on the other hand, causes us to feel contracted, not good enough, and needing to strive to get somewhere. When we are listening to The Guru, we feel like we are insufficient and need to do something to be good enough, valuable, worthy.

The ego is the only thing that causes us to feel contracted and insufficient, since that is not the Self's perception. We are loved by the Self, and our humanness and so-called imperfections, like everything else, are accepted and cherished by the Self. *Perfect* and *imperfect* are not in the Self's vocabulary. Such a categorization is a concept, like the concepts good and bad, which also have no reality. These types of categorizations belong to the ego. In truth, we are neither good nor bad, perfect nor imperfect; we just *are.*

Because the ego can't comprehend or even experience the Divine, the mystical, the ego often misunderstands and distorts the spiritual teachings it comes across. Since The Guru is the ego, and the ego doesn't understand the Truth, listening to The Guru's distortions and lies results in a lot of confusion for spiritual seekers.

Spiritual teachings are meant to guide seekers out of the egoic mind and into the experience of their true nature, but when spiritual seekers are firmly stuck in their egoic minds, the teachings are often misunderstood and then used by The Guru to make the seeker feel insufficient, and those negative feelings perpetuate ego-identification. The ego doesn't really want the Truth to be discovered because then the ego can no longer remain in charge. Discovering the Truth may not completely annihilate the ego, but it changes our relationship to the ego dramatically, and that change is felt like a death to the ego.

THE EGO AS THE PLEASURE-SEEKER

The ego is a security-seeker and a power-seeker, but it is also a pleasure-seeker, and that pleasure-seeking sometimes runs contrary to its other goals. Nevertheless, one of the ego's main personas is The Pleasure-Seeker. It's part of the ego's nature to avoid pain and seek pleasure, but The Pleasure-Seeker is a sensuous creature, and it's not as interested in avoiding pain as having pleasurable experiences.

The pursuit of pleasure comes in a number of forms. The most accessible routes to pleasure are food and sex, although food as pleasure is more of a phenomenon in affluent countries. Other routes are alcohol, drugs, and experiences that are considered fun, such as watching TV and movies, or experiences that are considered exhilarating, such as skydiving, riding roller coasters, and gambling.

The ego as Pleasure-Seeker is seeking a transcendent experience and relief from the suffering of the human condition, which ironically, the ego is the cause of. The pleasures of the flesh and other pleasures provide relief to some extent, but only briefly. These pleasures need to be experienced again and again because they provide only fleeting happiness and relief. Despite this obvious fact, the ego doesn't seem to see the truth about pleasure-seeking, and it goes back repetitively to things that provide only fleeting pleasure instead of looking for something more lasting and satisfying. The ego as Pleasure-Seeker is like a rat that is so consumed with pressing the lever that gives it food, that it doesn't consider other possibilities for its life.

When it's time to awaken, the aspect of the Self that is waking up from the illusion finally sees the futility of continually seeking fleeting pleasures, and it starts looking for deeper fulfillment. Once true happiness is sought, it can be found because this treasure isn't really hidden. True happiness has been available all along but simply not recognized. Many already know the secret to true happiness, and are freely sharing it with those searching for it.

The Pleasure-Seeker is behind all addictions. It might be more accurate to say that negative thinking and feelings are behind all addictions, since negative thoughts and feelings create the suffering that people are trying to rid themselves of when they turn to food, drugs, sex, and others things for pure pleasure. Behind every addiction are unmet, unhealed, feelings and negative thoughts about oneself, life, and others that need to be seen and seen through. The ego can produce a tremendous amount of pain by convincing us of terrible lies about ourselves and life. These thoughts and feelings can make life seem unbearable. Compulsions come from negative feelings that have been buried, and these compulsions initiate and maintain addictive behavior. Those caught in addictions usually need help identifying the negativity they have bought into and help moving beyond that negativity to a more positive perception of themselves and life.

The Pleasure-Seeker's voice is the voice of temptation: "What difference will eating another piece of cake make? It tastes too good to not have another. You only live once. I'll go on a diet next week." "Another drink would be great. Why not? Let's party!" The Pleasure Seeker goads us on and on toward more of the same pleasure, until that pleasure turns into pain. It prods us past the point of satiation to the point of pain or actual damage to the body.

The problem isn't seeking pleasure, because that's fine in moderation, the problem is that The Pleasure-Seeker is never satisfied. It doesn't know when to stop. The problem is also that when we are involved in pursuing pleasure compulsively, we aren't doing anything to uncover and heal the negative thoughts and feelings at the root of our unhappiness.

When we are identified with the ego as The Pleasure-Seeker, we actually aren't enjoying life very much, but running from the pain caused by believing the egoic mind. We aren't really happy, and we aren't really having fun. Addictions are anything but fun. The illusion is that our favorite pleasures are necessary for our happiness. For example, those addicted to food really believe they need their chocolate cake and other goodies to be happy. Giving them up seems unthinkable. The illusion that they need something outside themselves to be happy keeps them in the grips of addiction, and numbing their feelings out with their addiction keeps them from discovering the real cause of their unhappiness, and the solution.

THE EGO AS THE BUDDY

Another guise of the ego is that of a friend. This guise is experienced more positively than The Tyrant or other more negative guises the ego takes on, such as The Judge. When the ego can't get our attention by shaming us, scaring us, bossing us, or making us feel bad in some other way, it may take the guise of our friend. This is the most deceptive guise, really, because this guise can feel good and feel more like yourself than any other persona. It is the most benevolent form the ego takes: It chats with us like a friend. The kind of conversations we have mentally with the ego as The Buddy are similar to the conversations we might have with a real friend. The Buddy is the most positive side of the ego.

When we have evolved beyond listening to the negativity of the egoic mind, the ego as The Buddy is often what's left. Even though giving our attention to the friendly, chatty thoughts of The Buddy isn't likely to cause us to contract or feel stressed or tense, like identifying with other thoughts does, giving our attention to these useless thoughts means we aren't being more present to what else might be arising in the moment, such as intuitive messages or other possible communications from the Self. As long as we are giving our attention to The Buddy, we are still identified with the egoic mind, which means we aren't having as full an experience of the moment as we could be having. Furthermore, listening to The Buddy reinforces the habit of paying attention to the egoic mind, and doing that can quickly lead to giving our attention to some other less benevolent guise of the ego.

The voice of The Buddy is friendly, upbeat, supportive, conversational, and chatty: "I think you should wear the blue dress; you want to look your best." "Let's have lunch a little later so that we can take a walk first." "If anyone can get all that done, you can!" When we have seen through all the negative guises of the ego, The Buddy is the ego's only hope of keeping us identified with it. When the thoughts in your mind are primarily chatty, that's a good sign. The next step is to ignore even those. You don't need them. They only take you away from being more present to whatever you are doing and experiencing.

THREE STEPS FOR DETACHING FROM THE EGOIC MIND

The first step in dis-identifying from the egoic mind is to become aware of the thoughts that are going through your mind. No one can do this perfectly, as the thoughts are so many and can pass through so quickly, but any effort in becoming more aware of what the mind is telling you is a very big step in evolution. Most people have little awareness of what they are thinking. Some awareness of what you are thinking is essential in beginning to see what the ego is up to.

One of the values of meditation is that it trains you to notice the thoughts in your mind without identifying with them and responding automatically to them. Meditation helps lengthen the space of time between when a thought arrives in the mind and when you identify with it or respond to it. Once there is even the briefest space of time between a thought appearing in your mind and you identifying with it, that allows for the possibility of not identifying with it. For most people, there's no space of time between a thought arising and their identification with it, so there's no possibility for choosing to not identify with it until after identification has happened, and then that choice is often more difficult to make. The ability to catch a thought before identifying with it is a huge step in evolution. It opens the door to awakening, and once that door is cracked open, it cannot be closed.

Once you have some ability to notice your thoughts and to choose to identify with a thought or not to identify with it, then you actually have to make the choice to not identify with it. You have to choose to ignore that thought. Noticing your thoughts is the first step and the most important step, but noticing your thoughts isn't enough to become free from responding

automatically to them. Once you notice them, you have to choose
to ignore them, to not identify with them.

The two basic steps in detaching from the egoic mind are to
notice your thoughts and to ignore them. However, because
ignoring thoughts isn't that easy, since we are programmed to
believe them, there is an intermediary step, and that is to see that
a thought isn't true or valuable. Once you see that a thought is not
true or valuable, ignoring it is the natural consequence. If
someone is telling you a lie, and you know it's a lie, then you
naturally don't pay attention to it. With the egoic mind, you may
first have to see that a particular thought is a not true, not
meaningful, and not helpful, before you lose interest in it. We are
programmed to be very interested in our thoughts and to believe
that they contain information that is important to our survival.
Before we can easily ignore our thoughts, we have to see that this
isn't true. Our thoughts are not valuable, meaningful, nor do they
keep us safe.

You may need to observe your thoughts for quite some time
before you are convinced that they have little value and that they
don't contribute to your life or wellbeing. It can take a while to see
through the illusion that thoughts are important, meaningful, and
valuable. Even when you have seen through the illusion, you are
still likely to get caught up in certain thoughts.

Every time you become contracted, tense, and unhappy, that
means you have identified with a thought that isn't true, or is only
partly true. Any thought that causes you to contract doesn't serve
you or life. It isn't helpful. The ego keeps us imprisoned with
thoughts that make us feel bad, and then it keeps us involved with
the egoic mind further by offering us a solution to feeling bad:
have some cookies, try harder, get a makeover, make more money,
get a relationship. Those are the kinds of solutions the ego offers

to the problems it creates. The ego does whatever it can to keep us involved with it, but once we see what the ego is up to, the game can't really continue.

So the first step in detaching from the egoic mind is to notice your thoughts. The second step is to stop believing your thoughts are true and valuable, and the third step is to ignore your thoughts. The way you ignore them is to get involved with something else instead. You move your attention from thinking to *being*, to the experience you are having in the present moment. What are you experiencing right now besides a particular thought or feeling? Get involved with reality, with the present moment, for it will never come again.

NOTICE WHAT WANTS TO THINK

Exercise: Noticing What Wants to Think

Do this when you sit down to meditate or to just be quiet.

Notice how you want to think, how much you like to think. What wants to think is the ego, the false self; and what notices the desire to think is the Self. When you are having the experience of wanting to think, it really feels like you want to think, but in fact, it's just as possible to realize that the Noticer (the Self) is perfectly content with just noticing, just existing, just being. The Noticer also might impel you to get up and do something, but it doesn't use thought to do that; it just motivates you inwardly.

The Noticer, or the Self, is a more subtle experience than the ego, which is dominant in most people's awareness. The ego has a noisy, authoritative, sometimes pushy, and sometimes chatty and friendly voice that catches our attention, like a television or radio program might. We want to know what it has to say, even if the subject isn't really of interest, even if what it is saying is untrue or scares us or makes us feel bad. We are interested in what the voice in our head has to say to us. We *want* to listen to it. This is the programming. We are programmed to want to listen to our thoughts.

This is the programming that needs to be seen through to be free of the domination of the egoic mind, which isn't the wise helper and mentor it pretends to be. It doesn't have the answers for how to live life, although it pretends to. Fortunately something else does, but it doesn't talk to us like a person or the TV or the radio, in words, but more subtly. It "downloads" understanding and insight into our body, which show up as a knowing, and it impels us to take action in certain directions, wordlessly. We just feel moved, and that feels right.

The other thing that needs to happen to be free of the egoic mind is to fall in love with the Truth, with what is real and true right here and now. What is arising from your depths? What is present in the moment and can be experienced, besides thoughts and feelings, which are the products of the egoic mind? When we stop giving our attention to our thoughts and feelings, and we experience the present moment purely, we discover gratitude, love, contentment, and joy, just waiting to be noticed.

As we evolve as a species, these positive feeling states will become predominant, and the egoic mind will fall into the background or disappear altogether. This is where humanity is headed, and it will result in much happier people and a world at peace, once and for all. This is what falling out of love with our thoughts leads to, and all it takes is seeing that the desire to get involved with the egoic mind isn't a worthy desire. There's nothing in it for the real you or for humanity, only for the ego.

When we turn our attention away from that desire, we are gifted with everything we ever really wanted.

CHAPTER 4
Desire: The Fuel of Evolution

THE ROLE OF DESIRE

We can't talk about happiness without also talking about desire. The Buddha said that desire is the cause of all suffering, but that doesn't address why desire exists. Desire is an integral part of being alive in this realm. To say that desire is the cause of suffering doesn't mean it is bad. Desire is neither good nor bad. Desire is a driving force that brings about evolution, not only of the ego, but also of the Self.

Desires are as much a part of being human as having a body and a mind. Like thoughts, desires are part of our programming. They are not thoughts, but they are translated into thoughts and expressed as wants. They are experienced as drives, urges, impulses. Here is an exercise that will help you identify your desires and become more discriminating about them:

Exercise: Identifying Your Desires

This inquiry will help you discriminate between more meaningful desires and less meaningful ones. It will also help you uncover the role that certain desires play in your life. You may also become aware of desires you were not aware of.

Everyone has certain desires that keep appearing. What desires are prominent in your awareness now? Have they been prominent for a long time or are they relatively new or just passing through?

Which desires are shaping your life right now? Which desires are you following? How is that for you? Which desires are you not following? How is that for you?

Do some of your desires feel more meaningful than others? All desires are not created equal. Some desires, when followed, lead to deep satisfaction, but many lead only to more desiring. What category does each of your desires fall in?

Thoughts and desires go hand in hand to create the impetus toward action and, ultimately, the drama created by the ego that we refer to as *my life*. Desires propel life forward. They give our lives structure by giving us something to do. They give us a goal around which to mobilize ourselves. As a result of all this activity, we learn: We learn about ourselves, we learn to cooperate with others to get what we want, we develop skills for getting what we want, and we learn about the value of our desires. This is all grist for the mill of our personal evolution.

While we are learning and evolving, the Self is also learning and evolving. The idea that the Self evolves may seem strange if you are used to thinking of the Self as static and complete. But if that were so, why would the Self create other realms to explore? It delights in creation and exploration, just as we do, and all this experience can't help but evolve it. The purpose of creation, both ours and the Self's, is to fulfill curiosity: "What would it be like if...?" An idea arises to experience something, and circumstances are created to make that experience possible. What is experienced becomes part of the Self's understanding, and that understanding helps shape further creativity and exploration.

Part of the Self's creativity is the desire to explore all ways of being human and all types of human experience. To explore in this way, the Self has devised a way of programming human beings to ensure that every human being is unique. What would be the point of duplicating experience by duplicating creation? The uniqueness of every human being is the Self's creativity in action. The desires that arise in us are the Self's creativity at work to provide it with what it needs to evolve.

THE ROLE OF ASTROLOGY

The programming of the drives, which results in individuality, is accomplished through astrology. Astrology imprints us with the desires that make us unique. These desires are experienced as drives, and they relate to the twelve signs of astrology. For instance, the sign Cancer gives a drive for home, family, security, and preservation of tradition. Those imprinted with Cancer energy especially desire those things.

Everyone has a variety of signs in his or her astrology chart in addition to the sun sign, and therefore a variety of drives. Some of these drives are conflicting, and that produces challenges. Have you noticed how the Self likes challenges? They make for interesting twists and turns in the life story. Different combinations of the twelve signs in each chart and other factors create infinite possibilities for the Self to explore.

Drives are not the only story told through the astrology chart. The chart, which is a picture of the heavens at the moment of birth, tells how the drives will be used by the Self to achieve an overall goal, or life purpose, for that lifetime. For every lifetime, the Self generates a plan that includes a life purpose and certain lessons, and then it selects a time of birth that will provide the drives and challenges needed to bring that about. Exactly how this story will play out isn't known ahead of time because there are too many variables, which is part of the fun and learning for the Self.

The unique combination of drives in every chart allows the Self to explore the possibilities within each combination. Human beings are unique in the universe. Through humans, the Self is exploring a particular formulation of drives, physicality, mind, sensory capabilities, and emotions. What the Self learns as a result will be used to refine life forms and generate new ones.

To accomplish this adventure, a soul, which could be described as an offshoot of the Self, becomes cloaked in a body and personality, lives out the life story, learns from it, and following an interlude in nonphysical realities, returns to earth to learn some more. After hundreds of such lifetimes, the individual may be ready to awaken from the illusion and discover what has really been going on.

Not everyone is ready to awaken. Many are busy, and rightfully so, learning what they came to earth to learn. However, eventually, in this lifetime or in some other, the time will come to awaken. Before that, the soul's purpose is to live out its destiny, which is driven by desires. Those desires are the means for the soul's evolution and for the Self's evolution through that individual. These lifetimes are not a mistake. They are exactly as they are meant to be. They are a tool for the evolution of the soul and the Self.

Our desires provide the impetus for our life plan. For instance, if your life plan includes being a politician, you will be born when you can be imprinted with drives appropriate to that, such as a drive for leadership (Leo or Capricorn), a drive to communicate

(Gemini), and a drive to work on behalf of a cause (Aquarius). Further encouragement for that direction might come from being born into a political family or during an important time in political history.

Drives are difficult to ignore, and we aren't meant to ignore them because they are the means by which we evolve and unfold our life purpose. We are here to learn the lessons of having these drives and to learn to respond to these drives in ways that are beneficial to ourselves and others. The drives don't go away even after awakening because they are part of the personality pattern we are clothed in, which we need to function in the world.

After awakening, we still have a personality. We still have the same desires and drives, but we are less attached to having them met in a certain way. The Self intends to use these drives to meet its goals. So what changes after awakening is not the drives, but how they are expressed and *who* is guiding them. Before awakening, the ego is usually in control. After awakening, the Self is in charge, and the drives operate more spontaneously, without premeditation or planning. The egoic mind may still try to strategize its own direction, but that strategizing is recognized for what it is.

When the Self is in charge, we move smoothly from one activity to the next. What we do has an ease about it, even though we may be working very hard. Whatever the Self needs to fulfill its plan appears when it is needed. Without the egoic mind's confusion and conditioning, the Self can simply move forward with its agenda.

ALIGNING WITH THE SELF'S GOALS

Desires are the fuel of evolution, and yet they are also the source of suffering according to the Buddha, who was referring to the desires of the ego. The Self also could be said to have desires, or drives. But instead of causing suffering, they bring fulfillment, peace, and happiness. The Self is driven to fulfill a certain plan in every lifetime, and doing that brings a sense of rightness, freedom, and joy. These feelings are how we can tell when we are aligned with the Self's goals. Here is an exercise that will help you notice when you are aligned with the Self:

Exercise: Exploring the Feeling of Being Aligned with the Self

This inquiry will help your actions become more aligned with the Self.

Think of a time when you felt elated, fulfilled, excited, and joyful, when everything felt just right. What were you doing that caused you to feel that way? Those feelings are encouragement from the Self to do what you chose to do. They are how the Self expresses its gratitude to you for allowing it to have that experience.

The next time you have those feelings, notice what you are doing. That activity is an activity the Self is rejoicing in. It's saying yes!

Achieving the ego's desires gives a fleeting glimpse of happiness, while achieving the Self's goals gives deep and lasting satisfaction. When the Self's goals are being realized, the ego's desires don't matter. Have you ever been so inspired and excited by doing something that you didn't care whether you drove a nice car or lived in a nice house or had the other things the ego craves in this society? True happiness comes from pursuing what is meaningful to the Self, and that surpasses any happiness that gratification of egoic drives can provide.

Pursuits outside the Self's provide a hollow and impermanent happiness, but the Self allows us to pursue them anyway because doing so is part of our learning. We learn that getting what the ego wants only leaves us wanting more. Trying to fulfill the ego's desires is like trying to fill a bucket that has a hole in it. This is one of the great lessons of our many lifetimes. We learn a great deal from those pursuits, but those pursuits don't make those lifetimes happy and fulfilling, although other things, such as love, might. Only in our later lifetimes, when we become more aligned with the Self and its drives, do we begin to experience true happiness and satisfaction.

There's a good reason why pursuing the ego's desires doesn't satisfy: The egoic mind is programmed for dissatisfaction. It is made for critical analysis, and it's a particularly harsh critic. The egoic mind is the part of us that says no to the present moment. Nothing is ever good enough, at least not for long. Rejection of life goes on until we catch on that it is the egoic mind's job to say no. It's just doing what it was designed to do. If we listen to it, we will never be content because it isn't programmed for contentment. Here is an exercise that will help you notice the egoic mind's dissatisfaction:

Exercise: Noticing the Egoic Mind's Rejection of What Is

This inquiry will help you see how the egoic mind is constantly trying to change whatever is by finding fault with it.

Observe your thoughts as you go about your day. Pay attention to the egoic mind's commentary. How does it talk to you? What kinds of things does it say? Notice how it tries to improve things by rejecting and judging them. It is trying to be helpful, but is it? Mostly, you will find that the egoic mind judges, compares, evaluates, and complains. How does that make you feel if you listen to it? Is it a voice of wisdom and truth, as we so often assume? Or is it the voice of a petty complainer? Everyone's mind is programmed to judge and complain, but we don't have to become that voice. There is something wiser that doesn't speak in words. You are that!

Although the ego is continually discontent, something else is content in every moment, no matter what is going on. Unlike the ego, it is very subtle and quiet. This something, this contentment, is who we are. Contentment is a quality of the Self. When we are very still and not paying attention to the egoic mind's ranting, we can experience that contentment, but we have to want to.

It can take lifetimes before we decide to disregard the egoic mind and pay attention to the more subtle experience of the Self. When we do turn our attention to the experience of the Self, which can be experienced by being very present to the moment and not involved in thoughts, it can be known by certain qualities, most notably, love, peace, contentment, gratitude, and acceptance. It loves all of life and accepts whatever is part of any moment. That quiet acceptance is easy to overlook because it is so easily overshadowed by the egoic mind's loud insistence that everything is not okay. That great, loving okay-ness with everything the way it is, is what we are! And it has always been here.

The egoic mind creates the drama of life through its insistence that there is a problem that needs solving. This perception sets the wheels in motion toward a solution, and our life becomes about that. The Self accepts that as well. It allows whatever is happening, including the ego's rejection of what is happening and its attempts to fix it. The Self knows there will come a time when it will be realized and the Truth seen.

THE CAUSE OF SUFFERING

The egoic mind is the cause of suffering. Nothing more. Suffering only happens in response to a thought. We suffer because we think something about what is happening, what happened, or what might happen. We create a story about what is, what was, or what will be; then we suffer over it. We particularly suffer over fears, which are negative ideas about the future, although any idea can cause suffering if it is believed.

Even positive ideas can cause suffering. Something as simple as, "I'm doing great" can cause suffering because there will come a time when the egoic mind will declare, "I'm not doing great." Every positive thought has as much potential for suffering as a negative one because it carries with it the fear of losing what is desired.

In either case, whether we are thinking a positive or negative thought, we have thought the egoic self into existence. The *me* is created through thought. Before thought, there was no egoic self, only the Self. The birth of the *me* is the cause of suffering. The two go hand in hand. The *me* and its story is about separation, and separation is painful. Anytime the focus is on the *me*, we suffer, whether the *me* is being painted positively or negatively.

We suffer not only because we make ourselves separate from others, but also because we make ourselves separate from the Self. However, this suffering is not a mistake; it is part of the Self's plan too. *Suffering* is what wakes us up out of the egoic state of consciousness. It is not only grist for the egoic self's mill, but also a prod to awaken us to our true nature. Suffering is not a mistake.

Suffering is the result of our programming. We are programmed to have an ego that generates thoughts (including the *me* thought) that cause suffering. However, we are also given a way out of suffering. Life is like a puzzle: We are being asked to find the solution to suffering. We look here and we look there for the way out: Is eating the way out? Is being busy the way out? Is having more money the way out? Is being famous the way out? Is having the right relationship the way out? No, no, no, no, and no. We eventually discover that none of these things are the way out. Then what is?

After looking in all these directions and more, we begin looking into philosophies and teachings that might have the answer. Is psychotherapy the way out? Is meditation the way out? Is a vegan diet the way out? Is yoga the way out? Are affirmations the way out? No, no, no, no, and no.

When we are ready, a teacher appears who has found the way out. "You don't exist," the teacher says. "If that's the truth, I don't want to hear it," we say. And we go back to looking somewhere else. Finally, we run into the Truth enough times that it can't be denied.

What a shock. What a blow. No me. What now? How will life be lived? You don't know. You drop all pretense of knowing and just let yourself not know. Not knowing is the natural state. However, this not-knowing is not a place of *never* knowing. Knowing happens; it just doesn't happen ahead of time, but in each moment. Knowing unfolds from one moment to the next. Who knows about the next moment? We only know about the present moment. This is how life is lived without the *me*: from moment to moment.

USING THE MIND TO UNRAVEL THE EGOIC MIND

To begin to live in the moment more fully, we have to become aware of our egoic mind, what it is thinking, and how true those thoughts are. The good news is we don't have to do anything to develop that awareness. We have always been aware of our mind or we wouldn't be able to recount what is in it or think about our thoughts. Something else is present besides the mind that has always been aware of it and everything else that is occurring in the sensory mechanism we call our body. This awareness, this Noticer, this observer, is you, the real you.

Exercise: Noticing the Real You

The real you is subtle. This inquiry will help you become more aware of who you really are.

Who or what is it that is aware of reading these words? Notice that awareness. How do you experience it? What does it feel like? Where do you experience it? Is it contained anywhere? Just stay with the experience of it for a moment. This is who you are. The experience of who you are is available in every moment. All you have to do is give your attention to the real you instead of to the egoic mind.

The egoic mind projects another you, the thinker of the thoughts. This is the ego, the *you* that you think you are: The *you* that has a name and looks a certain way and is a father/mother, sister/brother, and so on. (Fill in the blank with all the things you call yourself.). That *you* is the one that does not exist. That *you* isn't real. Instead, you are the *awareness* of the person you think you are.

Once you see this, you have to wonder why it took so long. Programming. That's all. We don't see it because we are programmed to think of ourselves the way we do. There's no getting around our programming except by seeing that it's not the whole truth about who we are. We are programmed to believe an illusion. Once we realize this, the jig is up, as they say. The bell can't be un-rung, and we can't go back to believing a lie. We may still do some of the same things we did, but life is never the same.

However, our programming still has some pull. It can pull us in for a while, but not for long before we catch ourselves laughing for taking the *me* so seriously. We may find the ego endearing and silly, but we can't buy into its perspective for very long. Most of what the egoic mind says just doesn't seem true anymore.

What an amazing discovery! What a relief it is to discover that we are not this individual who suffers and struggles so. We can finally give up the effort to be somebody special, to know things, to be right, and to get it right. We were never satisfied with ourselves or others, no matter what we did or what they did. It was a no-win game. What a relief it is to give up the effort to be better, do better, and get more.

How did we miss the fact that everything we have ever wanted has been here all along? The peace, happiness, and joy we have been searching for, competing for, have been here all along in the space between our thoughts. We are that peace, happiness, and joy. We missed it because it is who we *are*. It is too close for us to see, like an eye that can't see itself. It is so ever-present that, like water to a fish, it is taken for granted and not questioned. Like the air we breathe, it is invisible and without dimension, and the ego doesn't pay attention to such things. The ego has eyes only for the tangibles in life.

Besides, the ego has been very busy creating a life, a story, by manifesting problems and then trying to solve them. When we were identified with the egoic mind, we were too busy to ask questions. We had a thought and then did something about it. That's what life was about. But once we begin questioning the egoic mind, the illusion begins to unravel.

When the time comes to awaken, the Self puts thoughts into the mind that question the validity of our other thoughts. The Self also draws others to us who realize the Truth and have seen through the egoic mind. Questions about the nature and purpose of life also begin to arise in the mind.

Until then, the tendency is to respect and adhere to whatever goes through the egoic mind. Like someone lost in the ocean who has just been thrown a life preserver, we cling to each thought for dear life. After all, without our thoughts telling us who we are, who would we be? We don't think that being no-thing is an option. To the egoic mind, being no-thing is the same as not existing. The ego would rather be anyone, even an unhappy someone, than not exist at all. This domination of the egoic mind is the cause of suffering.

FREEDOM FROM SUFFERING

When we are not identified with the egoic mind, but with the whole truth of who we are, the Self, there is no suffering. Once we realize the Self, we are still driven to do things, but the Self moves us effortlessly toward its goals. There is no suffering because we no longer spin stories about whatever is happening. Suffering doesn't come so much from following our desires and drives as from the stories we spin about that: "It's not good enough," "I'm not good enough," "Life isn't good enough," and on and on.

In the egoic state of consciousness, every thought, feeling, and action is seen as either good or bad; and that evaluation is felt to be true. The story told is never the whole truth, but it is assumed to be. We are forever spinning stories about ourselves and others and about the past and future. These stories cause us great suffering because they aren't true, or at least not the whole truth. We create an imaginary reality with these stories, and then we live in that imaginary reality.

Meanwhile, the Self allows whatever reality the ego is creating. It's perfectly willing to have whatever experience we choose. It enjoys learning from it all. It's fascinated to see how the story will play itself out. After all, that's why it created these forms in the first place: It wants to see how each individual with its unique personality and set of drives will live out its drama in the world. How will it interact? What conclusions will it draw? How will it see life? What will it choose? The Self is enthralled with its creation and joyously anticipates its every move.

When we awaken and our identity shifts from the ego to the Self, we feel the joy and love the Self has for itself in all its many forms. When we are no longer identified with the egoic mind, any judgments, evaluations, stories, or points of view that still arise in the egoic mind are seen for what they are, and they stop shaping our reality. As the Self, our reality is our true nature, which is love, acceptance, joy, gratitude, and boundless happiness.

HOW DESIRES CAUSE SUFFERING

Desires don't cause suffering. Desires come and go. They arise in the mind and then disappear. If that were all that happened, there would be no suffering. However, something else happens: attachment. Attachment happens as a result of a story we tell ourselves about a desire: "I will be happy when...." Desire is a drive, an impulse, that comes and goes; attachment gives that impulse fuel and makes it burn: "I want this because...." Thus, the story is born. The general story is that fulfilling our desires will make us happy and not doing so will make us unhappy.

Going after what we want becomes the prescription for happiness. The trouble is that the drug being prescribed is addictive and has little lasting effect. All we are left with is more craving. The more we pursue egoic desires, the emptier we feel and the more we think we need to fill that hole. All we really want is happiness, but we look for it in all the wrong places. We look for it in the fulfillment of our desires, but getting what we want only leaves us wanting more of that or wanting something else.

We become addicted to wanting and never question its value. We are so sure that something is going to satisfy us sometime, even if it hasn't yet: "The *next* million dollars will do it." Like a heroin addict, what we really want is our craving to end. We want an end to all this wanting and never feeling satisfied, but that will never happen by continuing to pursue our desires. It can take lifetimes of seeking pleasures, money, fame, love, beauty, success, perfection, and ideals before we are exhausted and see this.

The suffering from endlessly seeking and never getting enough is what eventually wakes us up from the illusion, which so often feels like a nightmare. Thus, desires play two roles in the illusion: Following desires maintains the illusion (the drama) through which the ego learns and evolves, and disillusionment with desires dissolves the illusion.

GIVING UP WANTING

Exercise: Noticing How Often You Want

As you are going about your day, notice how often your thoughts are about wanting something. What do you want? Does what you want change from day to day or stay the same? Do you have one particular desire that arises often, or do you have a number of desires? How strong are these desires? Are they a source of suffering?

Usually the mind is focused on one particular thing at a time, not everything in the world you might want. It may obsess about a relationship or a new sofa, a new job, or a new car. It may obsess about being successful or being thin. Sometimes the desires are relatively small—new curtains or a better stereo—but even desires like these can feel obsessive and important: You *really* want that!

The more we think about something, the more we want it. So even little things can seem more important than they are. The mind has an amazing capacity to focus narrowly, and when it does that, what it focuses on becomes magnified and disproportionately important. It feels like you really need that to be happy or to be successful or whatever.

Being something as a result of having something is really the issue. We don't want things just because they are nice; we want them because we feel they contribute to our *identity*. They make us feel more attractive, more successful, more special, or superior in some way, and that's why having them seems so important, no necessary.

The experience of getting what we want so often falls short of what we hoped it would be because we imbue objects and other things, such as a relationship or a particular job, with more value than they have. Objects and other things we want can't make us happier, and the feeling of being special they may provide lasts only briefly. The reason getting these types of things can't make us happy is that getting these things is the ego's idea of happiness, but the ego is in the business of producing unhappiness. So if you follow the ego's prescription for happiness, you will find yourself unhappy even when you do get what you want because the ego will come up with reasons to be unhappy with what you now have, it will want more of that, or it will want something else.

The ego is what produces unhappiness, and it accomplishes it through the thought "I want...." This seemingly innocent thought, "I want...," if believed and identified with repeatedly instead of ignored, takes us down the path of suffering until, we think, we get what we want. For some desires, that may be an awfully long time!

If thoughts of wanting served us in some way, it would be different. But they don't help create what we want. They come from a place of lack: "I need it to be happy, and I don't have it." Wanting and needing take us out of the present moment, where life is unfolding and bringing us exactly what we need. The ego doesn't believe that, of course. It doesn't believe that life brings us exactly the experiences, support, and people we need.

The ego's desires come in the form of thoughts of wanting, and they don't serve us or Life. What would it be like if you ignored your thoughts of wanting, if you pulled the plug on them? Life would still go on, wouldn't it? It would go on with much more acceptance and joy. You don't need those thoughts, and they take you away from what you really want. Once you see how useless those thoughts are, you will find it much easier to be present to life as it is showing up now.

Wanting is discontentment with what is, but it's just a thought of wanting. When you turn away from those thoughts, you discover that life is fine and unfolding beautifully just the way it is. Those thoughts give you a sense that you have a problem to solve, that you *have* to get what you want. But the truth is there is no problem and there is nothing you have to get to be happy. That doesn't mean you won't get things because, of course, you will get lots of things. But wanting them and thinking about them only gets in the way of appreciating and enjoying life as it is perfectly unfolding right now. Here is an exercise that will help you see the truth about your desires and detach from them:

Exercise: Examining Your Desires

This inquiry will help free you from the suffering caused by desiring.

What is something you desire right now? What is it you are telling yourself about this desire, that is, what do you believe fulfilling this desire will do for you? Is it possible that you already have what you really want right now even without fulfilling your desire? You can still pursue this desire, but if you are clear that the thing you want doesn't have the ability to give you what you really want, you won't suffer if it doesn't get fulfilled.

When we finally see the truth about our desires, we surrender. At first, this may feel more like giving up after being defeated. Eventually, that surrender is experienced more like a dropping into the moment, into the Real. When we finally give up on our desires, we send our egoic mind into retirement. What else does it have to do if we are not listening to its prescription for happiness?

When the egoic mind is quiet, something else can come forward with its agenda. It doesn't speak to us like the egoic mind does, though. It may not speak at all, but we feel it. We feel moved to do this and do that. We may not even know why, but we don't care. Doing it feels so right that we don't need a reason. The rightness is reason enough. The feeling is so simple, so clear, so unobstructed by thoughts, so free. All the identity that is usually attached to taking some action is absent. Before, when we did something, we imagined how others might react and what that might mean for our self-image. Now, we aren't spending time thinking about *me*. We aren't spending time thinking at all. Our actions are no longer centered on building an image that will keep us safe in the world.

As the Self, we are safety, we are peace, we are happiness, we are love—we are everything. We don't need to *become* anything because we already *are* everything. What a relief! At last we can just *be*. That is all we ever really wanted anyway. All the struggle and effort was just an attempt to be okay enough so that we could just be. We had to find out for ourselves that the struggle and effort were never necessary. Like Dorothy and her cohorts in *The Wizard of Oz*, we had what we needed all along! It was always possible to just be.

CHAPTER 5
Knowing and Not Knowing

THE IMPOTENCE OF THE EGOIC MIND

The egoic mind has us fooled. It's convinced us that it is powerful, which is exactly what it is not. The egoic mind has no power whatsoever. By itself, it has never been able to change a thing, least of all the present moment, which is all that really exists. Somehow we have come to believe that thinking something can make it so. But if that were true, life would be very different. As it is, by themselves, our thoughts and desires (which are just more thoughts) have never had the power to get us what we want. If they did have that power, we think we would be happy, but that is another illusion.

The ego throws the words "I want" and "I don't want" around like a king's declaration, as if saying them changes what *is*. The egoic mind acts like a king, an emperor, but the emperor has no clothes. If you pay close attention to the egoic mind, you will be surprised at how often those words arise in response to what *is*. All around, life is happening richly and exquisitely, and the ego is busy saying, "I want this" and "I don't want that."

We constantly evaluate our moment-to-moment experience, including our own thoughts about the moment. This evaluating, judgmental voice is the primary voice of the egoic mind. We hear this voice almost continually. Its judgments and evaluations are part of "I want" and "I don't want," because there are always reasons for wanting and not wanting, and those reasons are the judgment that something is good or bad. Notice how the ego has little capacity for subtlety or complexity. To it, something is either good or bad, black or white, and nothing in between. Here is an exercise that will help you notice how frequently and automatically the egoic mind generates judgments:

Exercise: Noticing Judgments

This inquiry will help you disengage from the egoic mind and realign with who you really are.

Notice how the egoic mind has an opinion about everything. Notice how having an opinion is even more important to the egoic mind than the content of the opinion. Often, any opinion will do.

Observe your thoughts while you are engaged in some activity. Notice how often your thoughts are judgments. Without even realizing it, we are often propelled by these judgments from one activity to another. This is not how life is meant to unfold, but the Self allows us to follow our judgments, to pursue our attempts to make things better, until we are finished with that way of structuring our life. The Self offers a more meaningful structure if we stop listening to the egoic mind and start listening to it.

Judgment is one cue that we are identified with the ego. It takes us away from the truth of who we are because to speak a judgment, is to speak a partial truth, which is a lie. Think about this: Is anything ever all good or all bad? Can you think of anything that doesn't have both positives and negatives? Even the death of someone we love can have deep positive consequences for our understanding. Growth, understanding, evolution, and love are not won easily in this world. Difficulties often precede them. However, the ego, whose measuring stick for everything is how it is for *me*, can't see so broadly. Seeing the truth requires something more real and true than something as imaginary as the *me*.

The *me* is in no position to evaluate something, and yet that is its job! The egoic mind is programmed to do little else but evaluate, but it is like a judge who doesn't have a clue about what is true. That evaluation, instead of improving our lives as it promises, only contributes to our unhappiness because it separates us from others and distances us from what is true and real.

What an interesting situation. The setup is plain: If we want to be happy, we have to see through the lies spun by the egoic mind. The trick is the illusion and lies are part of our programming, so they are not so easy to see through. Because the only thing capable of doing that is the Self, the only hope for true happiness is getting in touch with the Self.

WHO YOU ARE IS AN EXPERIENCE

"Getting in touch with the Self" makes the Self seem far away, but there is nothing closer. The Self isn't something we have to go searching for. We have always been alive as the Self, but the Self is very quiet and overlooked much of the time because the egoic mind is so noisy. Because our senses keep us focused on *things* instead of *experience*, we often miss the experience of the present moment, which is where the Self can be felt.

Exercise: Getting in Touch with the Self

This inquiry will help you experience who you really are.

Notice what is happening now outside of your thoughts. What are you experiencing in this moment? What are you aware of? That aware Presence is who you are. What subtle sensations are part of the experience of the moment? These subtle sensations are how you experience who you really are.

The experience of the present moment is subtle compared to thoughts and sensory experience. We get glimpses of it when we stop thinking for a moment. Experience is alive and well in between our thoughts. It is even present during thoughts, although it often goes unnoticed. We can't *not* experience because we can't *not* be aware. Awareness, consciousness, and experience are the same thing.

Who we are is not separate from experiencing. Who we are is more like a verb than a noun. It's more like *awaring* or *experiencing*. It's not a static thing. It's not a thing at all. It's no-thing. That's why it's so difficult for the mind to perceive. *The mind can't perceive what is aware of it.* The Self is what perceives the mind, so when we are perceiving the mind, we are perceiving the mind from the standpoint of the Self. We are identified with the Self instead of with the egoic mind.

This is the only standpoint where real happiness is possible. When we are identified with the egoic mind and its perspective, all we see is what it sees—separation—and all we experience is what it experiences: thoughts and feelings, which are part of the illusion it is creating and living in.

If we were not also the Self, we would be stuck in the illusion forever and destined to live it out indefinitely, like a character trapped in a plot with no happy ending. Fortunately, the truth is really good news. The truth, that who we *think* we are is an illusion, frees us to be who we really are, which is happiness, joy, love, and wisdom. Who we are is not a thing, but a be-ing. We are the *experience* of awareness, aliveness, joy, love, acceptance, gratitude, wisdom, and happiness. And that is what the experience of every moment holds.

THE FALSE MOMENT AND THE REAL MOMENT

It might seem like the egoic mind is experiencing the moment, but it only experiences its version of it. In a sense, there are two possible experiences of every moment: the moment as experienced by the Self and the moment as experienced by the ego. The ego's experience of the moment is struggle, conflict, effort, dissatisfaction, restlessness, and unease. The Self's experience of it is freedom, happiness, peace, acceptance, contentment, and joy. Either experience is possible in any moment, depending on whether we are identified with the ego or with the Self.

The ego's experience is primarily a mental one. It is also often full of feelings, which are mostly a response to thoughts. Thus, the ego lives in a mental and emotional world, one full of ideas, beliefs, fantasies, plans, hopes, opinions, memories, judgments, desires, and feelings. Every one of these thoughts leads to suffering if it is believed, since believing them and investing energy in them is like investing in a lie. How can investing in a lie bring true happiness? The best thing that can happen when we are invested in a lie is to find out it is a lie.

Most of the lies the egoic mind tells us are the trickiest kind because they have some truth to them. The best way to fool someone is to mix some truth in with the lies. If something is blatantly untrue, we aren't likely to believe it. But if it has some truth to it, we may not question it. The illusion is a clever one.

We also believe the illusion because other people believe it, and that's a powerful reason not to question it. Questioning it can feel like a matter of survival, and to the ego, survival is paramount. Questioning the programming is tantamount to revolution, and that is dangerous. To become free of the illusion takes tremendous courage and a willingness to stand alone, particularly at this time, when most people are deep into the illusion.

REJECTING WHAT IS

One of the cornerstones of the illusion is the belief that things should be other than the way they are in the present moment. This is the ego's basic stance: rejection of what *is*, rejection of reality. The ego rejects what *is* as if it has a say in it. It has an idea about how things should be and then declares that is how they should be, as if that matters to reality. It plays at being the master of fate, when it doesn't have the power to move a feather. When it fails at changing reality, it fumes and fusses, blames and scolds: "How dare things not be the way I say they should be!" Like a spoiled child, it rails against each moment.

The belief that things should be other than the way they are right now is the belief most responsible for the suffering on this planet. It is a lie. Things can never be different than the way they are right now because it's already too late for that. Life has moved on to the next moment, and that moment can't be different from what it is either. Life is just happening, and the egoic mind is saying no to it all. It argues with reality at every turn, but that doesn't change a thing. It only makes for a lot of unhappiness.

"But what about our actions?" you may ask. "We can change things with our actions. Shouldn't we try?" We are free to try to change anything we like, but there's no guarantee life will be as it *should* be as a result of those actions or that we will be happier when we are done. The ego is not a wise master at all. It's guided by a narrow vision: What is best for *me*. It doesn't see the whole picture, not even the whole picture of what is best for the *me*. We can follow its vision and change things, but without the right vision or reason for changing them, the result is not likely to be very satisfying.

The ego's goal is always happiness in some *form*: money, fame, success, power, love, beauty, comfort, a better this or a better that. But true happiness eludes the ego. Nevertheless, we learn from all this seeking, and we learn to make better choices. As a result, the desires that drive the drama usually become less selfish and less materialistic and more caring and altruistic. However, as long as the search is motivated by getting something for *me*, happiness will continue to be elusive.

Fortunately, all this seeking doesn't interfere with life, although it can make for a lot of suffering. The Self is perfectly willing to have whatever experience we choose. The Self waits patiently until the Truth is seen and the drama has played itself out.

The way out of suffering is to notice how often the egoic mind says no to what *is*. Notice how the ego brings its view of good and bad to every moment and instantly decides that it should be different. We allow that rejection of life to continue because we unconsciously believe that resisting life is a good strategy.

The ego is at battle with life, and attacking each moment makes it feel safe, as if it can ward off trouble by declaring what is wrong. The truth is that nothing is ever wrong with what *is*. The egoic mind arbitrarily defines whatever *is* as wrong. It makes the moment its enemy and then prepares a strategy for fighting it. This is how it creates the drama we call life.

This battle with life also serves the purpose of giving reality to the ego's unreal existence. The false self exists as someone who believes this and doesn't believe that, who thinks this is good and this is bad, who likes this and doesn't like that, who wants this and doesn't want that. The false self is born from this conflict with reality. What else is the ego but ideas?

The way out of the suffering caused by the ego is to see that resisting and arguing with what *is*, is a poor strategy and has only brought grief. How does it feel to be at war with life? How does it feel to see life as something to be beaten, controlled, managed, feared? Is that the truth? Is life, is the present moment, really so bad? Is there really something here that needs to be changed? What if the present moment were fine just the way it is? What would that mean? What would that be like?

THE EGOIC MIND DOESN'T KNOW NO-THING

It turns out that everything the egoic mind thinks it knows is not true. It thinks it knows how things should be. It thinks it knows what is good and bad. It thinks it knows what will make life happy. It thinks it knows what beliefs are true and false. All this knowing is a stance against life, real life. It's part of a strategy that fights and rejects the present moment. All this knowing creates the drama, disappointment, and suffering we experience when we live life in response to the egoic mind. All this knowing is just plain exhausting.

What is true if all this knowing is not? What's true is that we don't know. That's the big truth the ego keeps running from. Not knowing is very threatening to it. Knowing helps it feel safe. The mind can't know Truth (it can't know no-thing-ness), so it settles for what it can know: concepts, beliefs, opinions, judgments, fantasies, and dreams, all of which are made up. It can't know reality, so it makes up its own.

The trouble with this made-up reality is that nothing can satisfy like reality. Expecting concepts and beliefs to be satisfying is like expecting a fantasy of a dessert to be like the real thing. How can a fantasy ever satisfy? Reality is juicy and rich and alive, while the reality the ego creates is lifeless and dry. No wonder we are never satisfied when we are identified with the ego.

Concepts give the ego the sense that it knows. It wants to know because it wants to be safe and it wants to be right. Not only that, the ego believes its point of view *is* right, even when evidence fails to support that. Knowledge at this level of consciousness is seen as a means for supporting what is already believed. As we evolve, we become less attached to our beliefs and more capable of questioning them and using knowledge objectively. Until then, knowledge is manipulated to fit the ego's beliefs, or ignored if it doesn't.

Concepts and language help the ego function in the world but at a great cost. What is lost is the Truth, the truth about who we are. The Truth can't be divided into words and concepts. It can't be talked about without leaving out some of it. No words can adequately describe it. Anytime we say, "It is this," we have put it in a category, split it into pieces; but the Truth is not separate from anything. It resides in everything, and it expresses itself through everything and through no-thing. Everything is its body, its sense organs, its voice, its breath. It is all around. We can't sense or experience anything that is not the Self.

The division of the Truth into concepts creates a *me* and a *not me,* and the drama begins. *Me* is the primary concept, and everything else is experienced as either against *me* or for *me.* The ego loves the simplicity of that false premise, never mind that it is false.

No wonder we suffer; no wonder we are in conflict with ourselves and with everything else. Every ego is operating under a false premise, is convinced it's right, and deals badly with the consequences. When its assumptions turn out to be wrong, blame and retribution are the ways it deals with that. All the cruelty in the world is perpetrated from that state of consciousness. All the negative emotions—anger, sadness, jealousy, hatred, fear, guilt, and shame—are also the result of the ego's mistaken assumptions and false beliefs.

THE ROLE OF EMOTIONS IN EVOLUTION

Like desires, emotions perform two functions in evolution: They evolve us by creating experiences we learn from, and they create the hell that eventually causes us to wake up from the illusion.

Emotions are not experienced in the mind, but they are inseparable from it because they are created and kept alive by thoughts. Emotions are the products of thoughts and one way the mind mobilizes the body. By themselves, thoughts have no power to affect the world. Emotions are the link between thoughts and actions. They provide the juice, the fuel, for activity, and they help justify actions: "I feel this way, so I'm going to do this." Feelings are uncomfortable, and action is seen as a way to regain comfort, balance, and peace, even though that isn't necessarily the result.

When feelings are aroused in response to a thought, the body acts to reduce the emotional stress. For example, the thought "He shouldn't have left me" might evoke sadness and any number of reactions intended to relieve the pain of the emotion: crying, making phone calls, eating, writing a letter, hitting something. Some reactions will be more positive than others.

If that thought hadn't been believed, feelings wouldn't have been triggered. We can't control the thoughts that arise, but if we have enough awareness of them, we can stop and examine them. When we see that a thought isn't true (which is almost always the case, since thoughts by their nature are partial truths), a negative emotional or physical reaction is less likely. We still might take action, but that action is more likely to be productive than destructive if it isn't in reaction to a negative emotion.

The problem is we are not always aware of what we are thinking or willing to examine what we are thinking before an emotion arises. Furthermore, some emotions are generated by unconscious beliefs and seem to come from nowhere. We can learn to become more aware of our thoughts and to ask ourselves if a thought is true; but if an emotion is already present, bringing our awareness and acceptance to it is all we can do. When an emotion is present, it means that either a thought has slipped by our notice or something we are unconscious of has triggered it. In either case, acknowledging the emotion and letting it be there is the best approach.

If we allow an emotion to be there, it will show us something about itself. It will reveal the conscious or unconscious belief behind it. This is one way we can become free of our conditioning.

We can't get rid of emotions by denying them or pushing them aside, by pretending they aren't there. They will just come back another time, perhaps more vehemently. Instead, we need to be with what we are feeling like a gentle parent would be with a frightened child, because all emotions are driven by fear. If we bring a gentle, accepting, and curious attitude to the emotion, it will open up and show us what is at its core.

Often a deeper feeling is at its core, such as fear or hurt, and one or more mistaken beliefs. The layers of feelings within each feeling need to be seen and accepted as well as the beliefs underlying them. Doing this will free the energy to be used in more positive ways. All emotions have a gift of insight to relay. Emotions are messengers about the mistaken beliefs we hold, which gave rise to the emotion. Those beliefs need to be seen before we can become free of the emotion.

Once we realize the benefit of working with our emotions this way, we begin to welcome them as signs, or signals, that we are believing something, consciously or unconsciously, that isn't true. Every emotion is generated by an untruth. Seeing those untruths as they arise is key to waking up from the illusion. The illusion can't withstand close scrutiny. When we bring the light of Awareness to the untruths that uphold the illusion, the illusion dissolves. This must be done repeatedly, as each bit of untruth comes forward.

Emotions themselves are not a problem, and they are not the cause of suffering. They are really just sensations, but how we react to them often does create suffering. Emotions aren't good guides for behavior. They are, after all, born from false beliefs. We tend to treat our emotions as if they are the problem, however, because they feel like a problem. They are uncomfortable, so we want to get rid of them, and taking some kind of action seems like the answer, even though it may not be.

Just being with an emotion with acceptance and curiosity will allow the emotion to run its course. Like thoughts, emotions come and go. If we don't give an emotion energy by feeding it with more false ideas or by acting it out, it will return to nothingness, where it came from.

Emotions have no more reality than thoughts unless we give them reality. Yes, they have a physical component, unlike thoughts; but just as we can learn to let a thought be in our mind without identifying with it, we can learn to let an emotion be in our body without identifying with it. Here is an exercise that will help your emotions evolve and become less problematic:

Exercise: Befriending Your Emotions

Do this when you are experiencing an uncomfortable emotion.

Notice what you are feeling. Let yourself really experience it. If you find yourself thinking about the emotion or the experience of the emotion, go back to just experiencing it. Notice the sensations that are part of the emotion, both energetically and in your body. How many different sensations are there? Usually there are several, some pleasant and some not so pleasant. Notice all these sensations without trying to do anything about them and without judging them or telling stories about them or about the emotion. If you find yourself labeling the emotion and telling yourself something about it, notice that, and then return to experiencing the emotion.

Let the emotion and the sensations be there without trying to change them or make them go away. Observe them. Be curious about them. Instead of treating the emotion like a problem child, approach it like you would a lost child, with kindness and curiosity. Try dialoguing with it: What would it say to you if it had a voice? Why is it there? How is it serving you? What does it want? After staying with the emotion a while, do you experience other feelings? What would those feelings say if they had a voice? Stay with that experience until you feel a sense of completion. Usually, that completion will be signaled by feelings of softening, expansion, relaxation, and peace.

PRETENDING TO KNOW

Because knowing seems like a matter of survival to the ego, it has devised a number of strategies for knowing. Of course, since it's impossible for the ego to know to the extent it would like to, none of these strategies actually work. They only provide the pretense of knowing and actually interfere with true knowing, which comes out of being present in the moment.

One of the ego's strategies is generalizations: We draw a conclusion from an experience and then generalize to other situations in which knowing is impossible or not yet possible. For example, someone with a mustache cheated us, so we conclude that the person in front of us now, who has a mustache, isn't trustworthy. In drawing that conclusion, we might think we are being intuitive, but we are actually being influenced by our conditioning.

We do the same thing with emotions: We carry an emotion from a past experience into a new one and react to the new experience as if it were the old one. We rarely react purely to an experience. We carry with us countless conclusions, generalizations, from the past that not only interfere with perceiving the present situation as it is, but also influence how we react to it. Such conclusions keep us from being present to what *is*. We think we know what the moment is about, but we don't. Our conclusions and generalizations keep us in a made-up reality instead of in the present moment. They cast a veil between us and reality.

Judgment is another strategy for knowing. The ego pretends to know what is good and bad. Although life doesn't fit into such neat categories, that doesn't stop the egoic mind from doing this. Like generalizations, judgments close our minds to the present moment and cause us to live in a fabricated reality, where everything is either good or bad.

Judgments help the *me* feel superior and in control. If the ego knows what is good and bad, it feels safer, as if knowing this has the power to change reality. Judging makes the ego feel more powerful. But the ego is still just a lot of ideas, and a lot of nothing is still nothing.

Judging stems from the ego's feelings of weakness, insecurity, and fear. But because judging has no power to actually change reality, it only results in more insecurity and fear. Strategies that fail make us feel even more afraid, powerless, and insecure. Has judging ever made you safer or even made you feel safer? For example, does judging a bad driver ward off danger or make you feel safer? On some level, we think our judgments keep danger and problems at bay, but that is magical thinking. Rather than making us feel safer, judgments leave us feeling small, petty, unkind, and therefore not very lovable or safe. Like every one of the ego's strategies, judgments backfire. All judgments do is cause suffering by keeping us out of the present moment.

Another strategy is pretending to know what we need for life to turn out right. But how many times has something happened that you didn't want, only to discover it was a blessing? We don't really know what's best for us, but the ego pretends to. Even when we have had lots of experiences of life working out just fine regardless of what we wanted, we still cling to the belief that we know what is best. Other people may not, but we do.

We also pretend to know what is best for others, and we use judgments to try to change them. We think we are doing them a favor, without noticing that this strategy doesn't work. People only change when they are ready to. We act as if judging is our duty to the world. We're so sure that our version of reality is right. If the ego is anything, it's certain it is right. The truth is the ego wants whatever it thinks is best for the *me*. It may disguise this as concern for others and pretend to see a broader picture, but it doesn't know what is best for the *me* or for others because its point of view doesn't include the Self's vision.

Another strategy for knowing is blind faith: We just believe something. We think that if we believe something long and hard enough, it will be that way. However, our beliefs have nothing to do with what will be. Seeing that is complicated by the fact that every once in a while what we think is going to happen does, which reinforces our tendency toward magical thinking.

THE EVOLUTION OF THE EGOIC MIND

All this pretending to know and then discovering we don't is painful. It's painful to discover that life doesn't conform to our ideas and desires. Much of the time, it makes us angry. If we think people or things should be a certain way and they aren't, we feel angry. Behind most anger is this lack of conformation between what we think or want reality to be like and what *is*.

Instead of accepting that there is rarely conformation between our ideas and our desires and reality, we tend to put energy into trying to get the *right* ideas and desires. We think that if we just think the right thoughts and desire the right things, life will work out the way we want, and there's some truth to this: Some ideas and desires are truer and, when coupled with action, can result in a more favorable reality than others. For example, although affirmations by themselves don't bring about the reality that is being affirmed, they may help counteract a negative belief that is interfering with the desired reality. Once that negative belief is no longer limiting reality, a more positive reality can takes its place.

Nevertheless, our desires and beliefs by themselves don't create reality. Reality is what it is in any one moment. However, our desires and beliefs do have a profound effect on how we react, on what we choose to do, and ultimately on our *experience* of reality, of what *is*. Instead of experiencing reality, we often experience a version of it that our beliefs have created. We interpret the present moment, and that becomes our reality. We spin stories about our experience, and that becomes our truth. As we evolve, we learn the consequences of our desires and beliefs, and we learn to take responsibility for the experience created by them.

For example, if you believe that others are out to victimize you, because you have experienced that in the past, then you might assume you were shoved when someone bumps into you accidentally. You won't experience what really happened, but what you *think* happened, and that's what you will react to. Our beliefs create our *experience* of the moment, and that experience reinforces our beliefs.

We spend many lifetimes learning to refine our ideas, beliefs, and desires so that they work better for us. We learn to choose ones that are truer and more useful. The Self is actually involved in that process of refinement. Through experience, and particularly through suffering, we learn to use the egoic mind more positively and productively. The Self facilitates this by putting suggestions into the mind that will help it to evolve.

The Self is exploring our creative potential by giving us the free will to choose our beliefs and goals. We are free to believe the ego's perspective or something truer, and we are free to follow the ego's suggestions or something truer. We've mostly been talking about thoughts that come from the ego; but ideas from the Self occasionally appear in the mind, and they are much truer. The Self uses the mind to convey ideas that will help us live in the world with more ease. It also plants desires and drives that will help create the reality it intends.

Everyone receives ideas from the Self to some extent. As we evolve, this happens more frequently. The balance of ideas from the Self shifts as we evolve because we learn to disregard certain egoic ways of thinking that haven't proven to be helpful. Through experience, we learn to discern between thoughts that aren't very true and ones that are truer. Generally speaking, negative thoughts are less true than positive ones, which is why replacing negative thoughts with positive ones is usually a step in the right direction.

Ideas and drives that come from the Self are often disregarded when they don't coincide with personal or cultural conditioning because the lack of agreement with conditioning makes the Self's ideas seem risky. Following the Self's inspiration and drives requires courage because most people are operating from the egoic level and don't trust ideas that don't conform to that.

Going against conditioning may seem risky, but not going against conditioning is even riskier. When we give our attention to only our conditioning, we risk true happiness, peace, joy, and fulfillment. Living solely in response to the egoic mind is insanity because it means basing our life on falsehoods. It doesn't matter if others choose to do that. The question is: Does it work to live that way? Just because others aren't asking this question doesn't mean you shouldn't. If you know the way out of misery, do you go back to it just to keep others company? We have a responsibility to ourselves and to others to live the Truth once we see it. Besides, the rewards are worth it.

Many of you reading this are meant to wake up in this lifetime. If your destiny is to awaken, you will, and you won't care what others think. A part of you may care, but the drive to live the Truth will be so strong that other people's opinions won't stop you. There's nothing more fulfilling than doing what you came into this life to do, and for some, that means not only waking up, but also living from the awakened state and expressing your talents from there.

Awakening is not about *you*. It's not something you accomplish for yourself. It's for the rest of you, the rest of your Self, in the guise of others who are still caught in illusion. Many of you are here to awaken others once you awaken, and others have talents that will help in other ways. Awakening is not for *you*. It's not a prize you claim because the prize can't be claimed until you see that there is no *you* to claim it.

THE POWER OF NOT KNOWING

What all of this evolution is leading up to is embodiment of the Self in this physical reality. This may sound radical, and it is, but the experience of embodiment is very ordinary because it is our natural state and because the Self is what has been living through us all along. The only difference between before awakening and after awakening is that after awakening, we are aware that the Self is living through us. As long as we were not aware of that, the Self allowed the ego to dominate.

One of the biggest differences between the egoic state of consciousness and self-realization is our relationship to knowing. After awakening, the predominant experience is one of not knowing. We freely admit the truth: We don't know. We realize we don't know the things the ego pretends to know and that trying to know them only causes suffering.

Admitting the truth is such a relief. It's hard work pretending to know and having to come up with answers when there aren't any. What a relief to not have to know or be right! What a lot of energy that takes, and all it causes is conflict and separation from others. What a relief it is to just speak the truth: "I don't know." After all, we are not responsible for everything that happens, but pretending to know makes us feel that way: "If only I had known...." But the truth is that, in the moment, we didn't. Now we see that life is just happening as it always has, regardless of whether we pretend to know or admit we don't.

Once we realize the Self, knowing happens in a very different way. Although knowing sometimes comes in the form of a few words, it is more often experienced as a feeling of knowing. All of a sudden, a sense of knowing springs out of nothingness, often bringing a solution we would never have thought of. It arises in the moment, and thinking only gets in the way.

This knowing is accompanied by a sense of rightness and an *aha*. It feels soft and expansive, and it brings relaxation and a sense of letting go. This rightness isn't like the certainty of the ego, which feels tense and hard energetically. The certainty of the ego is more of a defensive or offensive posturing. When the egoic mind knows something, it's ready to go to battle with anyone who sees things differently. True knowing, on the other hand, fills us with a confidence that makes the support of others unnecessary. All that matters is that we know something is right for us in that moment.

The egoic mind wants to know everything right now, on its timetable. But true knowing doesn't work that way. With true knowing, we don't know until we do. Knowing arises when it needs to and not before. It happens when it happens, and we don't know when that will be. It has its own rationale for arising when it does, and that may not be as soon as we would like. To be comfortable with not knowing, takes trusting that everything happens in its own time.

Knowing in this way makes for much more ease. It is also more effective. Think of all the times you have taken action that was unnecessary or counterproductive just because you felt you needed to do something, even though you didn't know what to do. Waiting until we do know takes patience and a certain amount of trust, but we won't be wasting our time and energy in needless activities.

Living this way does require trust, but that comes with self-realization. Why wouldn't you trust your Self? If everything is an expression of you, what is there to be afraid of? What is it you could not handle once you realize the Truth? Besides, most of our difficulties are not created by the Self, but by the ego as a result of its mistaken perspective. Challenges still come up after awakening, but they are created by the Self for our evolution, not by the ego, whose thoughts and reactions reap constant suffering.

After awakening, suffering drops away. Challenges don't end, but they are accepted and embraced for the opportunity for growth they provide. The suffering brought about by the conditioned mind is nonexistent or minimal, and what remains are intense feelings of freedom, joy, happiness, acceptance, compassion, and gratitude.

CHAPTER 6
Waking Up in the Now

WHAT IS REAL

We have been talking mostly about what is not real, what the ego produces and pretends is real, such as thoughts, feelings, and desires. What is not real wouldn't be a problem if it didn't take us away from what *is* real, from the present moment, which is where true happiness can be found. What is real is what *is*, what is right here, right now, not what is *not* here right now, such as what should be, could be, or was. What is real is what is true about the present moment. What is real is the present moment, which is constantly changing into the next moment and the next. What *is* keeps changing.

What complicates this is the fact that part of what is real in most moments is thoughts. The *experience* of a thought is real; it's happening now. However, what happens in the egoic state of consciousness is that a false reality is created by giving our attention primarily to thoughts. When attention is given mostly to thoughts, the rest of reality is overlooked, as if it didn't also exist.

Part of the rest of reality of any moment is the input from our senses: colors, patterns, light, shadow, beauty, warmth, cold, sensations, sounds, tastes, and smells. Moreover, the reality of any moment also includes the essence of who we are: joy, peace, contentment, acceptance, gratitude, and love. Who we are is alive in the moment, and the qualities we exist as can be experienced in any moment. Who we are is joy, peace, contentment, acceptance, and love. When we experience who we are, we feel these positive feelings, and that makes for true happiness. When we experience who we are, we also feel a sense of presence and aliveness because that is how the energy of the Self is experienced.

To leave out so much of reality from our awareness by focusing on the egoic mind's stories or on what is not here in the present moment, such as the past and the future, leads to a very limited experience of reality, which feels hollow because it lacks the fullness that is possible. When I say that thoughts and desires are not real, I mean that they are not the whole truth and therefore lack truth. If you had some ice cream and all you could taste was the creaminess and not the flavor, it wouldn't seem like real ice cream because the full experience of ice cream would be lacking.

The same is true when we are identified with our thoughts: The experience of thought is not the complete, full experience of the moment. We miss a lot of reality when we are lost in our thoughts. Just as we can't enjoy ice cream that only has creaminess, we can't find real happiness in a moment consumed by thoughts. True happiness can only be found in the fullness of the moment. Any happiness that may come from paying attention to the egoic mind's limited reality is also limited.

TURNING AWAY FROM THE NOW

In the egoic state of consciousness, we continually turn our attention away from the fullness of the moment to the products of the egoic mind: thoughts, desires, and feelings. The ego is entranced by its thoughts and desires and the feelings that arise from them, and it has little interest in anything else. And yet who we really are is not the ego, but something more all-inclusive that includes the ego and its servant, the mind, and allows the ego to do what it does. Because the Self is so allowing, when we are identified with the egoic mind, reality outside the egoic mind doesn't seem to exist. Reality becomes what the ego thinks it is, and so we find ourselves living in a reality that includes only a small slice of what is real.

Just as we become engrossed in movie images and forget our surroundings, when we are identified with the ego, we become entranced by the movement of the egoic mind: its thoughts, feelings, and desires. This becomes our world, our reality. We don't notice the space, the nothingness, the emptiness between the thoughts, which is more real than anything the mind is able to experience.

Thoughts, desires, and feelings are part of the Now, and by themselves, don't take us out of the moment. However, in the egoic state of consciousness, we rarely allow thoughts, desires, and feelings to just come and go. Instead, we identify with particular thoughts, desires, and feelings and feed them with more of the same; and doing that does take us away from experiencing the moment fully.

For example, the thought "I can't find a job" arises in the mind. This may be true in the moment, but the ego tends to interpret thoughts globally, as if this particular thought means that you will *never* get a job. The ego mixes fear in with the truth and creates a problem out of something that is just true in the moment. "I will never find job" becomes a problem for the mind to chew on, and it's always looking for something to chew on. This so-called problem generates more thoughts that attempt to solve the problem: "I'll look in the paper. Maybe I need to move. Maybe I should go back to school. Maybe my old place of employment has an opening. Maybe I should change careers." Any one of these thoughts may or may not coincide with what the Self chooses to do next. The Self will allow the ego to pursue any of these avenues in an attempt to solve the problem. Meanwhile, the Self will move as it always has to unfold the life, and what that will be won't be known until it happens.

In a sense, there are two things going on in any moment: what the ego is propelling us to do and what the Self is propelling us to do. Life goes smoothly when these drives are the same. But when they don't coincide, the result is confusion, discomfort, fear, anger, and sadness: suffering.

The ego tells stories about feelings too, not just about thoughts. For example, anger arises about something someone said. Instead of just allowing the anger to be there without doing anything about it, including thinking about it, the ego is likely to generate more thoughts: "He shouldn't have said that about me. He's a jerk. What does he know? I never liked him. That's so unfair." Those thoughts, in turn, generate more feelings: "I can't stand that guy. That really hurts after all I've done for him." Then those feelings might lead to actions: "I'll show him. I'm going to give him a piece of my mind."

Following our thoughts and feelings keeps us very busy and leads to a lot of suffering. It creates the drama we call *my life*. However, life doesn't have to go in the direction of our thoughts and feelings. That isn't the life intended by the Self. It intends a different story, a simpler and potentially happier and more fulfilling one. However, the Self allows us to create these dramas and learn from them until we tire of them and begin to question the cause of our suffering.

Of course, desires work in the same way, and they are compelling figments of the egoic mind. For example, let's suppose you have a desire for a relationship. This could spur a number of actions that might keep you very busy: joining a dating service, calling up old friends, looking in the personal ads, going to bars, and fantasizing. However, if it's not time for you to have a relationship, according to the Self's plan, those actions aren't likely to bring one, although they are bound to bring some learning and possibly some suffering. The Self allows you to create this drama because this experience is part of the Self's exploration through you.

When our actions are not aligned with the Self's timing and plan, we spend time doing things that don't work out well and that often result in suffering. On the other hand, if something, such as a romantic relationship, is part of the Self's plan, the Self will bring it about in its own way, and the ego couldn't stop it if it wanted to. Life happens naturally and easefully when we are living the life the Self intends for us.

The mind is really just a mechanism, a tool for thinking and perceiving for the physical body, and as such, it serves the body well. However, reality is much more than what the mind and senses are able to perceive and sense. And yet we take ourselves as the mind and the ego, and our world as what our senses tell us about it.

Nevertheless, our senses do bring hints of something else. Many are able to feel the energy of the Self. As we evolve, we develop the ability to sense more of reality. We become more sensitive psychically and more capable of sensing outside our usual senses. For those whose senses extend to the more subtle aspects of life, the Self is very real indeed, more real than thoughts and things.

However, to the ego, beliefs, opinions, judgments, hopes, fantasies, fears, the past, the future, and almost any *thing* is more interesting than no-thing. The ego is likely to be more interested in, for instance, the style of a piece of furniture than how life is unfolding in the present moment. It doesn't recognize that something is happening in all of this no-thing-ness that has little to do with it, which is why it isn't interested. The ego is only interested in things that pertain to its story and its survival. It won't even be interested in something like furniture if furniture doesn't have some relationship to its identity, story, desires, or survival. The ego is not interested in everything, only in what will enhance it in some way.

As a result, the ego turns its attention toward what it feels may help it survive or be happier. It's a good thing it is interested in happiness because that desire for happiness is what ultimately causes the ego to be open to looking in directions it wouldn't ordinarily look, such as spiritual practices.

KNOWING IN THE NOW

Exercise: Discovering What Is Here

Do this whenever you want to get in touch with what is true:

Just sit still a moment and experience what is here, now. What do you experience? A thought? A sensation? An image? A feeling? A desire? Tension? Relaxation? Contraction? Expansion? Awareness? Presence? Silence? Acceptance? Beauty? Love? Joy? All that and more can be happening in the Now. It turns out that the Now is packed! If we don't follow our thoughts, feelings, or desires but just stay present to them arising and falling away, we will be able to experience everything else that is happening in the Now.

All of that experience packed into the Now is life living itself. Life is perfectly capable of carrying on, and it does, without so much thinking going on. Of course, some thinking is necessary to function and some is just fun, but most is extraneous and causes suffering. When we live in the Now, life is simpler. The egoic mind complicates life by creating problems that don't exist and then trying to figure out how to solve them. It offers everything it has learned from experience or read or heard from others that might be relevant. It is like a computer with lots of information, most of which isn't applicable to the present moment.

When we are very present to each moment, what is needed becomes apparent. The information offered by the egoic mind isn't necessary because the present moment already contains what we need to know, for now. This knowing keeps changing because the moment keeps changing, so how could the egoic mind possibly keep up with this? The egoic mind's knowing is stagnant and hit or miss at best, although sometimes the ego's knowing does coincide with the moment-to-moment knowing. When that happens, the egoic mind is reinforced.

We don't seem to trust that life is fine without the egoic mind's intervention. We really believe the egoic mind has something valuable to contribute because it convinces us that it does. But it doesn't. Outside of using the mind for functional purposes or for some fun, such as crossword puzzles and other mental games, the mind can be set aside. Once the Self begins to live more fully through us, the mind is taken up when needed and set aside when not. This new relationship to the mind doesn't happen overnight, however. We usually need repeated experiences of life happening just fine without listening to the egoic mind before we begin to trust this way of being.

More often than not, the egoic mind has failed us. But instead of giving up on it, we tend to keep going to it for answers. But they aren't there! The egoic mind has never had the answers we are really looking for. It only has answers to the most basic, practical questions. We are so sure we can come up with the answer to anything if we think about it long enough, but the egoic mind isn't equipped to tell us how to live life. The only good answers for that come from the knowing that arises in the moment.

Think of all the times you have struggled to figure out what to do about something. This can go on for days, even weeks or months, before you finally realize what to do. Where did that realization come from? Did it come from all the thinking you did? Usually it appears out of nowhere, when we aren't even thinking about the issue. The experience of knowing in the Now is instantaneous, sudden, sometimes surprising, and unaccompanied by thought. Inspiration, creativity, inventiveness, understanding, insight, and new ideas pop into awareness out of nowhere. That is the Self at work.

This experience is very different from thinking. Thinking is an experience of being absorbed in an imaginary reality: We picture what will happen if we do this or that. We might have an inner dialogue or conversation with ourselves about it. Perhaps we make a mental list of possibilities. All of those activities are taking place in our mind.

Knowing in the Now, on the other hand, happens when we are *not* thinking. That is the difference. The other kind of knowing is more like trying to know by thinking about something. These two kinds of knowing feel very different energetically and experientially. Once we are aware of the difference, they are not difficult to distinguish.

ACTING IN THE NOW

Knowing is not the only thing that comes out of the Now; so do many of our actions. Some actions come from the Now, and some are a response to the ego's thoughts and feelings. Both types of actions are going on simultaneously in most people's experience.

The ego is very focused on doing: "What should I do? What will I do? How will I do it? When will I do it? What will happen when I do that?" The ego takes on the task of planning the doing, motivating the doing, and evaluating the doing. It also wonders about the doing, imagines and fantasizes about the doing, worries about the doing, changes its mind about the doing, talks about the doing, and gets confused about the doing. The only thing the ego doesn't actually do is the doing, because the ego doesn't exist. It doesn't have a body to perform the doing. It tries to motivate the body, but the body is not the ego. The ego uses the mind, but the mind is not the ego.

The ego is simply thoughts arising out of nowhere, with no one attached to them. There is no person thinking those thoughts, only a body-mind having those thoughts and the semblance of a person. The person, however, is really only thoughts about a person. There is no actual person that is the ego. The ego is a sham. It's imaginary. It's no more substantial than a thought.

When we are identified with the ego, we are very busy planning and thinking about doing, and we are very busy doing what the ego suggests we do. All this doing causes our life to happen and to be experienced in a certain way. It shapes and creates a sense of self, and it constructs a life. The life the ego creates is based on its desires, its tendencies, and other conditioning, or programming. The person you think you are and the life that person creates come out of conditioned, or programmed, thoughts. But that's not the whole story, thankfully.

Because the ego doesn't actually exist, there must be something else here that does, and there is of course. What actually exists is the real you, the Self, and its consciousness inhabits (although not exclusively) your particular body-mind. This consciousness motivates and guides you, and it uses the body to speak and act. It operates alongside of the ego. It allows the ego to move you, while it also moves and guides you in its own way. While the ego primarily uses thoughts (the egoic mind) to move us, this consciousness uses intuition, inspiration, inner drives, and urges to move us.

When we are responding to the Self, it doesn't feel like the doing of the ego. It's fluid, natural, spontaneous, and without resistance or thought. We just act or speak spontaneously, and it feels right and natural to do so. Acting without effort or resistance is what spiritual teachers refer to as the experience of there being *no doer*.

When our doing is full of striving, trying, worrying, stress, and confusion, those actions are coming from the ego; when our doing is spontaneous and natural, those actions are coming from our true nature, the Self, and the experience feels like we aren't doing anything. It feels like going with the flow. It feels like something else is carrying us along (and it is), and we are just flowing with that without resistance. Rather than the egoic mind pushing us, we are being carried along, without any desire for things to be otherwise, without questioning the experience, without confusion: without thought. The experience feels right, so there is no need to *do* anything but go along with it.

The ego uses desire and fear to motivate us, which is stressful: "Will I get my desires met, or will what I'm afraid of happen?" However, with the Self, there is a deeper Will at work, one that is also shaping all of life. When we are aligned with that Will, we are aligned with all of life and in the flow. We are carried along. Our only job is to pay attention to where the flow is going, to notice it and adjust our course accordingly. We feel the rightness of our course with our Heart, and the mind is only used in practical ways: to read, calculate, learn, analyze, and so on. Doing arises naturally out of the flow as needed, and because those actions are part of the flow, they don't feel anything like the doing of the ego. The experience is one of there being no doer, yet doing is happening.

Everyone experiences this flow of action on a daily basis, at least briefly. We all move back and forth between effortful, ego-driven doing and effortless, Self-driven activity. And everyone is evolving toward living more in the flow. The more aware you are of the difference between these two types of doing, the easier it will be to move into the flow and stay there.

After awakening, most of our actions flow spontaneously from the present moment, although we may still find ourselves acting on our thoughts, desires, and feelings some of the time. This isn't a problem for the Self. It works with and adapts its plan to whatever we create on the egoic level. Besides, some of the thoughts, desires, and feelings we respond to come from the Self to motivate us to unfold its plan.

The Self has a number of motives for spurring us to action besides the intention to unfold its plan. For one, it enjoys playing in the material world. That is, after all, one reason for taking on a physical body. For the Self, life isn't only about learning and growth, but also about pleasure, fun, adventure, and discovery. Activities that provide these experiences nourish and expand the Self and us. The Self motivates us toward them by creating a desire for them when appropriate. After awakening, we enjoy life not only because we can handle challenges without suffering, but also because we allow ourselves to play.

When we are identified with the ego, play is often about escaping pain. It is often an attempt to feel good, or at least to stop feeling bad. After awakening, play, re-creation, is more about contacting the joy of being alive. This is the joy the Self takes in creation. Yes, the Self enjoys difficult situations for what can be learned from them, but it also savors the joys and pleasures of being in a body. It enjoys beauty, sensuality, eating, movement, singing, dancing, creating, and thinking. The Self derives great pleasure from those activities, and it instills a drive for them in us when appropriate.

The Self also motivates us to take action on behalf of others. It frequently helps itself, in the form of others, when the need arises by inspiring us to help. That drive doesn't come from the idea that we *should* help. Instead, it arises spontaneously from the Now. We do something just because we can and because there's a need, without any thought of reward or of what's in it for *me*. That type of action is unencumbered by thoughts, feelings, and attachment. Our actions feel easy, natural, right, and joyful. That joy and ease is a sign that our actions are aligned with the Self.

There's no shortage of drives and action coming out of the Now. The Self has lots to do in the world, which becomes very apparent when we stop filling up our lives with ego-driven activity. Activities that come out of the egoic state of consciousness are not nearly as fulfilling as those that come from the Self. The egoic state of consciousness has its place in life, but life doesn't start to become truly fulfilling and happy until we begin to live in the Now, where the Self's drives and joy for life can be experienced.

DOORWAYS INTO THE NOW

By now, you might be wondering how to get to the Now from the egoic state of consciousness. It's a very short trip: Just stop. Stop and notice what is here, right now, in the present moment. Noticing is the primary doorway into the Now. The others are variations on noticing that involve the body and senses: noticing beauty, noticing sounds and the absence of sound, noticing the breath, and noticing the body's sensations and energy. The body and senses play a key role in bringing us into the Now because full engagement with our senses precludes thinking. We can't think and be fully involved in our senses at the same time.

NOTICING

If you notice, you will see that happiness is already here. Still, no matter how good life may be, the ego says no to it: "It would be better if...." "I will be happy when...." As long as we don't follow those thoughts, we will be happy. But usually we give our attention to the ego's rejection of what *is* instead of to what *is*. We give that *no* the power to steer our actions: We jump from one idea to the next, trying to make life and ourselves better.

We will never arrive at happiness by listening to the *no*. Happiness just is. It is inherent in the moment, in the Now, in the form of joy, acceptance, and love. It can't *not* be. We only have to notice what already *is*. That's the only reality there is, so why waste your attention on what is not?

We think that someday there will be no more *no*, no more ego arguing against reality, and then we will finally be happy. But that day will never come. If you wait for the *no* to disappear, you will be waiting a very long time.

We don't have to get rid of the *no* to be happy; we just have to see it for what it is, the programmed discontent of the ego, and ignore it. The ego will never be happy, but we can be happy if we don't give our attention to what the egoic mind says we need to be happy. The ego doesn't know about happiness. What can it know about happiness? Its job is to manufacture unhappiness, and it's very skillful at convincing us otherwise.

Once we see this, the egoic mind has no power to draw us away from the Now. The only power it has is the power we give it by believing what it tells us. Now that you see this, there's no excuse for giving your attention to your thoughts. Pay attention to the present moment. Notice. That's all it takes. The price of admission into the present moment is attention.

This price is easy to pay because we are always paying attention to something. Attention is one thing that is constant; it's always happening. Attention is like the eyes of the Self. Where you are placing your attention is where the Self is focusing part of the Awareness that it is. The Self could be described as an *aware-ing* presence. It is sometimes simply called Awareness or Presence.

Your attention, which is part of Awareness, is directed either by the Self or by the ego. In any moment, the Self may be directing our attention or the ego may be. The Self allows attention to be hijacked by the ego because that experience is part of the Self experiencing the world. Even when attention is being focused by the ego, the Self remains aware of that. Awareness is never lost, but the ego is not aware of Awareness. After awakening, our attention may be briefly captured by the ego, but awareness of the Truth remains.

What we put our attention on is what we identify with. Attention directs identification. When we put our attention on thoughts, we become identified with them. And when we notice what else is here, now, in addition to thoughts, identification shifts from the ego to the Self. Here is an exercise that will help you be in the Now, where it is possible to experience the Self:

Exercise: Noticing

Try applying this to every moment!

Turn your attention to the present moment and notice what's happening right now. Is the ego saying no to that? That could be one of the things that is happening in the present moment. What else is happening right now? what sensory experiences? what thoughts? what judgments? what feelings? what insights? what desires? what urges? What is coming out of the moment right now? Something is always arising from the moment, and something is always being taken in by you. What is happening right now? Notice how the egoic mind tries to co-opt the moment, and then bring your awareness back to your sensory experience and everything else that is coming out of the Now.

BEAUTY

Beauty is the visual doorway into the Now, where we find the Self. We can enter the Now through the sense of sight, and the easiest way of doing that is by becoming absorbed in something beautiful. It is possible, however, to enter the Now by looking, really looking, at anything. Everything is part of the Self, and becoming fully engaged with anything brings us to the Self. Beauty may be the easiest visual doorway because we are generally more willing to become fully engaged with something beautiful than with something that isn't. We say yes to beauty, and that yes takes us into the Now. However, anything we see that we don't reject can bring us into the Now.

Looking at something beautiful opens the Heart. By that I mean that beauty can cause an expansion of our energy field that is felt as an opening in the area of the chest. This energetic reaction is a sign that we are in the Now and aligned with the Self. The Heart is like the heart of the Self. It is where the Self connects with the human and how it communicates with the human part of itself. More will be said about this in the following chapters.

Beauty connects us instantly with joy. Think of some of your happiest moments. The beauty of nature was probably part of many of your happiest moments. Spending time in a beautiful, natural setting is one of the easiest ways to get in touch with the Real, with the Self. Natural beauty brings us into the moment because it captures our attention so completely. The egoic mind has difficulty competing with it. Setting the egoic mind aside is much easier in a natural setting because a merging of energy fields happens that stops the mind. The life force in nature is so strong that it pulls us into it and right into the Self.

Many artists are drawn to creating beauty because of its power to bring us into the Now. A painting of nature can have the same effect as nature itself. However, art doesn't have to represent nature to evoke the Self; any expression of beauty can. Color, in particular, often has a powerful effect on us. The right combination or balance of colors can strike a chord within us that brings us Home.

Very detailed artwork has a special ability to bring us into the Now because the mind says yes to the detail. It loves getting lost in detailed designs and patterns, which act like meditational focus points. When the mind attends to color, detail, or pattern, it becomes still, and we drop into the Now, our natural state.

Exercise: Getting Back to the Now by Seeing

This is especially easy to do in nature.

Choose something beautiful to look at. Give it your full attention. If evaluations, labels, or other thoughts come up about what you're looking at or about anything else, bring your attention back to just seeing. Receive the visual impression and experience its impact on your being. How does the experience of seeing without thinking feel energetically? That peace is who you are!

Alternately, move your gaze from object to object, without letting it rest on any one object. This is an especially good practice for when you are walking in nature. Keep your eyes moving around the environment. If thoughts arise about what you are seeing or about anything else, notice them, and then go back to seeing and to experiencing the impact seeing has on you energetically.

LISTENING

Listening is also a doorway into the Now. Just as it is possible to enter the Now by really looking at something, it's possible to enter the Now by really listening to something. As with seeing, really listening to something is often easier when what we are listening to is beautiful to us, such as a piece of music, a bird's song, or a child's laughter. Beautiful sounds bring us into the Now because it's easy to say yes to the Now when what's coming out of it is beautiful to the ears. Beautiful music opens the Heart, and we land in the Now. Those who meditate to music or use it as part of their spiritual practice are well aware of this.

When we are listening, we aren't thinking because we can't

listen and think at the same time. So on the most basic level, listening brings us into the Now because it stops the egoic mind and puts us in a receptive mode. A natural surrendering to what *is* happens when we listen because sounds are what is happening, at least in part. Even attending to a part of what *is* can bring us more fully into the Now. Listening helps us get our foot in the door of the Now, and then once the egoic mind is quiet, we can give our attention to whatever else is happening in the Now. Listening helps train the egoic mind to be quiet and receptive.

Learning to be receptive is key to being in the present moment. The egoic mind is anything but receptive. It's too busy pretending to know to be receptive. Being receptive takes humility and surrender, which are not characteristic of the ego. Surrender, however, which is akin to acceptance, is the nature of the Self. Surrender is saying yes to whatever is, and that acceptance is the essence of the Self.

Listening to silence is a particularly powerful way to enter the Now. When we are attending to silence, we are attending to the Silence, the Self. The silence in between the thoughts, in between the words, and in between the sounds is where the Self can be found. We can learn to tune in to the energy of the Self during the silence between thoughts, words, and sounds. When our attention is on anything else, including sounds, we experience the energy of that instead of the energy of the Self. Once we are familiar with the Self's energy, if we put our attention on it, we will land immediately in the Now.

The experience of the Silence is peace, contentment, acceptance, gratitude, love, and joy. These pleasant states are not very interesting to the egoic mind, which likes drama and trouble because that gives it identity, a reason for existing. When the ego touches the Silence, it turns away from it—nothing is happening there! But the ego is so wrong. Life is pouring out of the Silence. That's where everything real comes from. But what is real is too complete for the ego; nothing is left for the ego to do. When we are in the Silence, we feel complete, and yet, life still happens: An impulse or urge arises from the Silence, and we follow it. The Silence may seem empty, but it's full of life.

Exercise: Getting Back to the Now by Listening

Sounds and silence are always available, so you can do this anywhere and anytime. You don't have to be sitting still.

Listen to the sounds around you. Receive the sounds without mentally commenting on them. If you catch yourself thinking, bring yourself back to listening. If you find yourself resisting a sound, such as a barking dog, notice that and then bring yourself back to listening.

Alternately, listen to the silence in between the sounds and in between the thoughts. What do you experience energetically? If you catch yourself describing what you are experiencing mentally or thinking about something else, notice that and then return to the experience of silence. Stay with this experience a while without rushing off to do something else or follow a thought. Notice how pleasurable it is. That experience is who you are!

THE BREATH

Paying attention to the breath is a time-honored way of returning to the present moment and to the Self. Meditation on the breath quiets the egoic mind, just as focusing on anything does, and a quiet mind enables us to experience the Now. Like focusing on sounds, focusing on the breath is possible in every moment. We don't need any special equipment to return to the Now!

Whenever we find ourselves mentally engaged, we can bring ourselves back to the Now by noticing our breath. Staying focused on our breath for even one minute can shift our state of consciousness. Notice when you are feeling tense, worried, fearful, angry, sad, or contracted and just give your attention to your breath. When you are contracted, it means you are giving your attention to a thought that is generating negative thoughts and feelings. By simply shifting your attention from that unreal experience to the real experience of the Self breathing you in the present moment, your consciousness shifts. Who is it that has been breathing you all this time?

Exercise: Breathing Your Way Back to the Now

This is especially helpful when you feel tense, fearful, worried, sad, angry, or any other uncomfortable emotion.

Notice the experience of breathing. Notice the feel of the breath as it enters your nose and leaves your nose. Without changing how you breathe in any way, notice how the body breathes rhythmically in and out, effortlessly, softly, gently. And there you are in the Now. If you find yourself thinking about your breathing, your body, or anything else, bring your attention back to the experience of breathing. The more you practice this, the easier it becomes to move into the Now, and the more you will want to.

THE SENSES

The expression "Stop and smell the roses" points to the importance of just noticing and experiencing the world through our senses. The physical world is continually affecting us through our senses, and the energy of other living things is continually affecting our energy field. Being in the Now means not only smelling the rose, but also seeing the rose, feeling the rose's life force and beingness, and ultimately, recognizing it as your Self.

Because the entire world is the Self, a full experience of any aspect of the world will bring us into the Now and into the experience of the Self. The Self delights in experiencing itself. That's one reason it has created the physical world. Through it, it is experiencing itself in various forms. We make it possible for the Self to explore and experience the physical world. We're like sense organs that allow the Self to experience itself through creation.

When thinking is not in the way, we are able to fully experience what's coming in through our senses and through a sixth sense, which senses the energy of every life form. This sixth sense is an extension of our physical senses. The sixth sense is not that mysterious, but the ego distrusts it because what the sixth sense senses is not perceived by our other senses.

When we pay full attention to what we are experiencing through our senses without the egoic mind's interference, we have a full experience of the Now. Our senses have the capacity to bring us into the Now instantaneously. This happens all the time, but usually we just as quickly withdraw our attention from what we are experiencing through our senses and go back to our mental version of the moment.

For example, when you see a rose, most likely you experience its beingness and the fullness of the present moment for only a split second before your mind comes up with a label: "rose." Then the egoic mind is likely to describe and evaluate the rose according to its perceptions and values: "It's past its prime and a little wilted on one side. It has a bent stem, and one leaf has been eaten by bugs. It's not pretty enough to give someone. " The mind's ability to observe and evaluate the physical world serves us at times, but not when it's applied constantly to every moment.

After labeling, describing, and evaluating the rose, the ego might launch into a story related to roses: "People came from all over to see my grandmother's rose garden." The ego has little interest in the actual experience of the rose. The rose is just one more thing that either serves or doesn't serve its story. The stories the ego usually tells are ones that reinforce some aspect of the ego's identity. This particular story could enhance one's sense of being special for having a grandmother who excelled in gardening. Or if the identity is a negative one, the story might be: "I can't grow a thing. I'm absolutely incompetent when it comes to gardening."

Regardless of what story is told, the result is the same: a feeling of hollowness and emptiness, although the ego quickly turns away from that truth because it would be fatal to its existence. If we paid attention to the impact that our stories have on our energy field, which registers them as contractions, we would recognize that they don't fulfill us. But since we usually don't stay with that experience any more than with the experience of the rose, we just keep telling stories in an attempt to get fulfillment from that.

We will never find fulfillment in trying to get the ego to feel good. The ego is programmed to not feel good. Doing things to try to make the ego feel good is a strategy that can never succeed. In the egoic state of consciousness, nothing that is sought after is ever enough to make us truly happy. Fortunately, no seeking is needed to find true happiness, only an end to seeking.

Exercise: Using Your Senses to Get to the Now

You can do this exercise anywhere and anytime. It's especially helpful when you find yourself caught up in the mental realm.

What's coming in through your senses right now? What are you experiencing? A sound? A sight? Something touching you? Warmth? Coolness? Air moving? Tension? Pain? Pleasure? Many sensations are likely to be happening at once. Notice them without labeling them, evaluating them, or thinking about them. If you find your mind doing that, bring your attention back to the experience your senses are bringing you. Experience whatever you are experiencing without judging it and without trying to hold on to it or push it away. Let it be the way it is. Experience what it's like to be a receptor. How does that feel energetically?

LOVING WHAT IS

Staying in the Now is the issue once we get there. We all dip into it many times throughout the day, but few stay there for very long because the egoic mind rejects the Now almost immediately. It says no to the stillness and peace of the Now because it has no interest in those states. It also says no to other aspects of the Now. For example, if anger is part of the moment, the ego says no to the anger by thinking about it and drumming up more feelings instead of just *experiencing* the anger. Thinking about a feeling is actually a way of rejecting the feeling because thinking takes us away from the experience of the feeling, and the experience is the real thing.

All that is really needed in a moment when feelings are arising is to experience them fully. Then that leads to something else in another moment: an action, a release of feelings, or maybe an insight. The ego, on the other hand, handles feelings the way it thinks they should be handled, usually according to conditioning. This is likely to have a different result than just staying with the experience of the feeling. The ego rejects the experience of the feeling, and in so doing, rejects how the Self is unfolding life. Instead, the ego attempts to make life happen some other way. The Self allows the ego to do this, but the price is suffering.

Let's take another example. In the moment, you are experiencing the tree outside your window and appreciating its beauty. Then your egoic mind comes into the moment and decides the tree should be pruned. Dissatisfaction and tension arise, as you consider how and when that will be done, who will do it, and how it will be paid for. In an instant, your ego turned the experience of the tree into a problem to be solved.

Trees do need pruning from time to time, but so much of what the ego drums up to do is unnecessary. It makes needless demands on things to be better according to its ideas. If the tree really does need pruning, the idea will arise out of the stillness of the Now, and action will be taken without a lot of resistance or thoughts. The things that really need to be done get taken care of by the Self without resistance. However, the ego doesn't trust this natural process.

If you pay attention to your egoic mind, you see that it's almost always in a mode of rejecting what *is*. Even after self-realization, that's what it does and continues to do because the egoic mind is programmed to do that. When we are identified with the egoic mind, its voice seems true. So when it says no, we agree. It takes dis-identification from the egoic mind to recognize that the ego is leading us down the wrong path. Once we have some detachment from the egoic mind, the ego's antics are pretty obvious. Even then, however, it takes practice to stay detached from the egoic mind from moment to moment and to keep our attention on the Now.

The opposite of rejecting the Now is accepting it. Just as noticing takes us into the Now, allowing keeps us there. Noticing and allowing go hand in hand. To be present to the moment, both noticing and allowing are needed. If you want to stay in the Now for more than a flash, you have to allow whatever is happening. You have to say yes to what *is*, and to do that, you have to continue to notice what *is*, which keeps changing. If you stop noticing, you are likely to find yourself back in your egoic mind because the mind quickly takes control of attention whenever it wanders from the Now.

What keeps attention from wandering is a genuine curiosity and love for the Now, for the Self, for the Truth. We have to want the Truth more than we want anything the ego might dangle in front of us. At a certain point in our evolution, the drive for the Truth becomes greater than the attraction of the egoic mind, and then we begin spending increasing amounts of time in the Now.

Curiosity and love are really the same thing. When we fall in love, we are infinitely curious about our beloved. And when we love an activity, such as a sport, a hobby, or a line of work, we are curious to learn everything about it. We can't tear ourselves away from what we love. That's how much we have to love the Now in order to stay in it.

We have to be willing to stay long enough in the Now to get to know it and fall in love with it. And for that, we need to have a drive to know the Truth. Our curiosity needs to be so great that we have to know the Truth. Where does that drive come from? It comes from the Self, of course. The ego doesn't want to know the Truth. At first, the ego might want to know the Truth because it thinks that discovering the Truth might enhance it. But when it finds out that isn't the case, the ego runs from the Truth and from the Real, the present moment.

There comes a time in everyone's evolution when the Truth must be known, when the drive for the Truth is so great that it can't be sidetracked by anything. Before that, we may have many experiences of wanting to know the Truth a little bit, as long as it doesn't demand too much from us. The spiritual path is an experience of dipping our toe in the water of Truth many, many times until we are ready to take the plunge. When we do, things are never the same.

It's no wonder the ego shies away from self-realization. Self-realization plunges us into the unknown without our defenses. We are stripped bare and left with nothing but living moment to moment. Who knows what the next moment holds? We don't know anything anymore, except when we do, but we are happy! What a surprise!

SAYING YES TO WHAT IS

Saying yes to what *is* doesn't mean you have to like what *is*. You only have to be willing to let things be the way they are, for now. This is a lot easier to do when you see the whole truth about something and not just part of it, as the ego does. The whole truth is that every experience has both positives and negatives and that whatever *is*, is constantly changing. Whatever we don't like, or like, about the present moment won't exist at some point. No two moments are ever the same. Even how we feel about what *is* changes. Feelings are another part of what *is* that we don't have to like; we just have to allow. Saying yes to what *is* just means allowing the way things are in the present moment to be the way they are.

Instead of calling this allowing, we could call it acceptance, but the word acceptance implies a degree of resignation. Acceptance, as it is being used here, just means telling the truth about what *is*. And the truth is that what *is* just is. That's all we have to accept. We accept that what *is*, is the way it is. We can't change the fact that we might prefer something to be other than it is, and we don't have to. Preferences are the way they are. A preference for something to be other than it is, is just one of the things to be accepted, allowed.

Our preferences are just part of the ego's programming. If we don't give our attention to them, they disappear. Have you ever wanted something really badly and then given up on it? That desire just disappeared, and you were no worse off. To be in the Now, we don't have to give up our preferences; we just have to give our attention to the truth, which may be that what we would like to be happening isn't happening right now. That doesn't mean that what we would like to happen might not happen in another moment, but it's not happening now.

The ego is like a spoiled child who wants what it wants right now. We can calm the ego by simply turning our attention away from its demands and bringing our attention to the present moment, which is full and rich and satisfying. The now has everything we need to be happy. What a wonderful discovery after so many weary years of desiring things and never being satisfied by them!

CHAPTER 7
Striking up a Conversation with Your Self

COMMUNICATION THROUGH DRIVES

Some drives come from the ego and some come from the Self. All drives manifest as an urge or impulse toward action. However, action on behalf of the ego is likely to be very different and have very different results than action flowing from the Self. Most people's actions are a mixture: Some flow from the ego and some from the Self.

When we are identified with the ego, it often co-opts the drives of the Self. When that happens, the actions still reflect the Self's drive, but those actions may not be the same as what the Self intended. Nevertheless, the Self allows this because we learn from this experience. For example, if you experience a drive for beauty, your Self may be motivating you to create art, but your ego may focus on making yourself more beautiful because physical beauty is so highly prized in our culture. The Self learns about beauty and evolves the aesthetic sense regardless of which avenue is followed. Not every action has to come from the Self, nor would that be possible. Actions coming from the ego are only a problem when they interfere with the Self's goals. When that happens, we miss out on fulfillment and experience only limited happiness.

Actions that are motivated by the Self and not interfered with by the ego have a rightness, spontaneity, and ease about them. They just happen. We get an idea and just do it, even if it doesn't enhance our security or status. Ego-driven actions, on the other hand, although they might also fit the Self's goals to some extent, have some motive of ego-enhancement.

This motive is how we can tell the difference between ego-driven actions and Self-inspired ones. Actions that come from the Self are done for the joy of doing them. These actions are intrinsically rewarding, and we do them even if they don't enhance our safety, status, comfort, or security. There may even be a cost to doing them, but we feel compelled to do them anyway. This is very different from ego-driven actions because the ego weighs the costs carefully and only acts when it sees a benefit for the *me*.

When we are aligned with the Self's goals, motivation is strong because what we are doing feels so right and is so intrinsically rewarding. To others, the intensity of our motivation may seem like obsession, but it isn't the compulsiveness that is often part of ego-driven activity. Compulsions are driven by repressed feelings, usually stemming from a traumatic experience that left a sense of unworthiness. Compulsiveness is an unconscious attempt to compensate for a lack of self worth or stave off a fear.

While Self-inspired activity is marked by satisfaction and fulfillment, ego-driven activity is marked by a sense of never having enough. Ego-driven activity is an attempt to get satisfaction and fulfillment from something that isn't capable of providing it, so those actions are doomed from the start. They will never bring happiness. This doesn't mean that ego-driven activities aren't worth engaging in, but we shouldn't expect them to bring us lasting happiness.

You have undoubtedly encountered people who are on fire with motivation, who stop at nothing to accomplish their goals. They are filled with excitement, enthusiasm, courage, and determination to do what they feel moved to do. They inspire awe in us because of what they are able to accomplish. Much of what we call greatness comes from being aligned with the Self. Being in touch with our true nature and doing what we came into life to do makes us feel alive, vibrant, energized, fulfilled, complete, and deeply happy. Fulfilling the life purpose is profoundly satisfying, regardless of what the life purpose may be.

A hallmark of the Self's goals is that they are beneficial not only to us, but also to others. The ego's goals, on the other hand, are more personal, less universal, and less far-reaching than the Self's. This doesn't mean that everyone's life purpose makes a mark on history, but our life purposes do touch others' lives in a positive way, even if only those close to us.

You see, the Self is very big, it includes everything, so its goals do too. Only the ego tends to focus narrowly on itself. The Self sees the ego as an instrument for exploring and serving all of life, all of itself, and not an end in itself. The ego, on the other hand, sees itself as the center of the universe.

COMMUNICATION THROUGH FEELINGS

Feelings are messages about desires and drives, either from the Self or from the ego. Most feelings are generated by the egoic mind in response to a belief or a desire. Feelings operate in conjunction with thoughts and desires, not alone. Whenever we experience a feeling, a thought or a desire is behind it. For example, the belief that you should be able to do something when you can't or the desire to do something when you can't might cause sadness, disappointment, and anger. Any mistaken belief or unfulfilled desire can have a similar result: Feelings are triggered, and those feelings trigger more ideas and more feelings: "This shouldn't be happening. If it weren't for him, I'd be able to do that. I hate feeling this way. I hate him." Instead of accepting reality the way it is, we argue with it by crying, getting angry, blaming, and feeling bad.

We are used to thinking of feelings as an expression of suffering. However, they are also often an unconscious attempt to manipulate reality, as if yelling or crying hard enough can change the way things are. Even feeling guilty or sorry can be a way of unconsciously trying to manipulate reality: "If I'm really good and never do that again, maybe things will work out." Some of this comes from religious upbringing that implies that if we're good we'll get what we pray for.

Again and again, the egoic mind sets us up for disappointment. It's amazing that we continue to believe it when it fails us so miserably. But instead of blaming our thoughts or desires for how we feel, we blame the situation, as if it could have been different. When we finally turn to look for the mistaken belief or the desire behind what we are feeling, that's a very big step in our evolution and a big step toward awakening. We are beginning to see through the illusion: the ego is fabricating a false reality!

We can learn a lot from our feelings about the role our beliefs play in our suffering. Our feelings call attention to our mistaken beliefs and make it possible to become free of those beliefs if we are willing to examine them. Usually, we don't examine our thoughts. We aren't used to seeing our thoughts as the problem. We think that the solution to feeling better is to change something outside ourselves.

Instead of looking for the mistaken belief behind the feeling and either changing or ignoring it, we try to change reality to fit our beliefs. And that's a prescription for suffering. We aren't that powerful. Reality does change—it is constantly changing—but how it changes isn't under our control, at least not completely. The Self is the ultimate creator of reality, and the ego is the co-creator only to the extent that the Self allows the ego to be.

The assumption that our thoughts and desires have the power to create the reality we want is a key misunderstanding that helps perpetuate the illusion. We believe that if we plan enough, learn enough, want what we want enough, work hard enough, and are good enough everything will come out the way we want. If things are not that way yet, we assume we just need to plan harder, learn more, want what we want more, work harder, and be better.

So is that your experience? When you do everything right, do things always come out the way you want? Instead of blaming ourselves for not being able to make life happen the way we want, we can just notice that no one else has ever succeeded at making life happen the way they want either. Reality is what it is, and it unfolds mysteriously, in part in response to our thoughts and beliefs and actions, but mostly according to the Self's plan for us and for its broader vision. Reality is exactly as it is meant to be, and only our thinking keeps us from appreciating reality as it is.

The ego resists seeing this basic truth because, once the truth is really seen, the ego loses its power and is returned to its rightful place as servant of the Self. The game is over, the ego lost, and we win. However, when we are identified with the ego, seeing the truth doesn't feel like a win. To the ego, seeing the truth feels more like a death, so it feels very dangerous. That's why we run from this realization, we deny it, we don't see it. Seeing the truth is too threatening, to the ego anyway.

Fortunately, we are not the ego. We only *think* we are. So when the ego is dethroned, we are free, not dead. Who we thought we were still exists, but now we see that who we thought we were is just a bunch of thoughts that make up this character, *me*. That is really the only difference. But this changes everything: We no longer believe the egoic mind. We stop living from the egoic mind and begin living from the Heart.

The suffering created by listening to the egoic mind eventually brings us back to the Heart, which has been participating in life all along, attempting to guide and mentor the character we have been playing. Once we stop listening to the egoic mind, it becomes easier to hear the Heart, which speaks in many different ways, including through certain positive feelings.

While most feelings are generated by the egoic mind, some feelings come from the Self. However, feelings from the Self aren't emotions, such as anger, fear, and sadness, but positive feeling states. The most obvious feelings the Self uses to communicate its plan are elation, joy, excitement, and happiness. Such feelings are a sign that we are aligned with our plan. They give us immediate feedback about our choices and actions. We can trust these feelings, but there is one catch: They are also present to some extent when the ego gets what it wants, but with a subtle difference.

The difference is in how those feelings are experienced. When elation, joy, excitement, and happiness come from the Self, they are long-lasting and bring with them peace, contentment, satisfaction, and fulfillment. In contrast, when elation, joy, excitement, and happiness come from the ego, they are short-lived and have a giddiness about them, like the high from a drug. When the ego gets what it wants, visions of grandeur and a better future often swirl about in the head. The ego doesn't rest in peace and contentment, but generates more thoughts and desires.

There's also a set of feelings that signal when we are *not* aligned with the Self. Those are the feelings that belong to depression: sadness, hopelessness, wanting to die, lack of motivation, and unhappiness. Those feelings may also be present in the midst of tragedy or when the ego doesn't get what it wants. The difference is in how long those feelings last and whether they are associated with circumstances.

Deep, long-lasting depression is a sign that the Self's plan is not being fulfilled. The Self uses feelings of depression as a wakeup call to get us back on track. This kind of depression doesn't necessarily coincide with circumstances. In fact, some successful people are deeply depressed because their success isn't bringing them the fulfillment they long for. On the other hand, when those feelings result from a tragedy or disappointment, they usually only last until the situation changes for the better. Depression is common when we lose someone we love or when other life-altering events happen, but depression of this nature disappears with time and changing circumstances.

If you feel depressed and there is no obvious reason, it may be useful to daydream a little and ask yourself: What would I be doing if there were no limitations? Usually we stop ourselves from following our dreams, our Heart, by erecting limitations, which often come in the form of self-defeating statements. Often a *should* is involved in these statements: "I can't do that because I should...." The egoic mind often interferes with the Self's goals by holding certain beliefs. When our beliefs are keeping us from following our Heart, depression might be the way the Self is communicating to us that we are off track.

Underlying most depression is anger at frustrated goals. When a frustrated goal belongs to the Self, it's important to identify that goal and do something about it. When that goal belongs to the ego, it's also important to identify it and determine whether it is of real value. Sometimes the Self frustrates one of the ego's goals because achieving it would interfere with its goals. Not getting what we want can cause us to feel very angry with life, when life is just trying to bring us to a different avenue of happiness, one that will bring truer, more long-lasting happiness.

Depression is often a message that the Self has plans for us that aren't being followed. It's a wakeup call for a new life, for new possibilities we may not have allowed ourselves to consider. Depression may be trying to steer us in another direction. Discovering what needs to be included, or excluded, in our life to be happy may take a lot of examination and honesty, but doing what it takes to discover this is always worth it. Fortunately, the Self is continually communicating its plan in many different ways; so, if we are at all willing to listen, we will pick up the clues we need to lead us to greater happiness.

COMMUNICATION THROUGH OTHERS

The Self communicates its plan not only directly to us, but also through others. It uses itself in the form of others to help unfold its plan. We are, after all, instruments for the Self in this physical world, and the Self will use others to help it accomplish its plan, which includes not only each of our plans, but also an overarching plan for all of humanity. Life isn't only about what can be discovered through these bodies and personalities. Another story is being unfolded, and that is the story of this world. The Self has a global plan as well as individual ones, and our individual plan fits into the global one.

The ego can't see the big picture. It can't see what the global plan is and how it fits into that plan. It has a different agenda, one that is often very different from the Self's. But that makes life interesting. It creates the drama and unpredictability of life. Without the ego, there would be no challenge, no antagonist to create the drama. The Self is enjoying the interplay of itself with creation. It created the ego to do exactly what it does. The ego is no mistake. The Self created the illusion, and the Self is waking up from it one person at a time. Meanwhile, the Self is enjoying the game of life.

One of the main ways the Self wakes itself up is others. People wake up, and then they wake others up. That's how it works. Those who have seen through the illusion are in a position to help others see through it. However, the Self not only communicates through those who are awake, but also through everyone, regardless of their degree of ego-identification.

The Self is constantly talking to itself through other people. Think of all the times someone has told you something that turned out to be valuable to you. Maybe he or she suggested a book or told you about a class or introduced you to someone who became significant to you. We need others. They enrich our lives in so many ways, and not just those we deeply love; even acquaintances and people we don't like often have something important to share with us.

The Self literally uses the minds and mouths of others to communicate. If the Self wants us to know something, it plants that idea in someone we encounter and inspires that person to share it with us. This experience is common to all of us. Without even thinking, we find ourselves saying something to someone. "Where did that come from?" we wonder. Indeed. Where does any thought come from?

Thoughts arise seemingly out of nowhere, sometimes from the unconscious mind, where conditioning lies, and occasionally from beyond that: the Self. Thoughts that arise from the unconscious mind are often paired with feelings and take the form of opinions, judgments, desires, preferences, and stories about the past. They are nearly always about the *me* and tend to be repeated, like a broken record, regardless of what is actually happening in the moment.

A communication from the Self, on the other hand, pops into our mind and out of our mouth before we have a chance to think about it. Speaking just happens, and it feels like we didn't have anything to do with it. The communication is clean, with no sense of *me* taking credit for it. This way of communicating feels pleasantly surprising because the message is delivered so freely, generously, and with openness and love. Delivering a message from the Self feels good.

If you pay attention, you will begin to notice how often that happens when you are around others. When we are really present to people and not busy thinking, it can happen more often because our channel to the Self isn't clogged up with our own thoughts. When we aren't thinking, our mind is in a receptive mode and can receive the Self's communications more readily—and speak them. If our ego isn't busy communicating its own agenda, our mouth is free to communicate the Self's.

COMMUNICATION THROUGH EVENTS

Accidents, illness, the loss of a loved one or a job, natural disasters, and other life-altering events are another way the Self may communicate its intentions. Events such as these may be used to shake us up out of our usual way of thinking and being in the world and bring us into greater alignment spiritually. They often help us see what is real and of true value and what is not. They often help us get in touch with what really matters in life, as the ego's petty concerns are put in perspective.

Such incidents may be calls to either wake up out of the illusion completely or out of part of it, out of some misunderstanding. They often bring some awareness, particularly of the preciousness of life and the impermanence and unimportance of the ego's goals.

Not all events are wakeup calls. Some are self-created and provide the lessons that help us evolve on a personal level. For instance, if you lose your job because you weren't responsible, that is a lesson in responsibility. Or if you lose your spouse because you were unkind, that is a lesson in love. Many of our difficulties and failures happen because we are unwilling to comply with something or because we lack some understanding, and loss may correct this. Reaping the results of our actions is called karma.

Karma is often called The Great Teacher. It brings us the circumstances we need in order to learn something. Some of the lessons come immediately and some come in other lifetimes. Immediate karma is easier to identify than karma we are meeting from a previous lifetime. Usually there is a sense of fate to the latter: The situation couldn't have been avoided, and we did nothing apparent to cause it.

Car accidents are one way of illustrating the difference between immediate karma and karma from another lifetime: If a car accident is caused by you through inattention, that's immediate karma, and the lesson is to pay attention. If a car accident is unavoidable and not caused by you, the accident may be your karma from a previous lifetime coming to roost, although the accident may be part of some other lesson. There is one other category: accidents that are caused by someone else's karma.

The Self isn't always able to prevent an accident from happening, although it will try if it isn't part of our karma to experience it. In some cases, the Self's only means of preventing accidents is to speak to us intuitively, and if we don't hear or respond to that intuitive message, the Self can do nothing else. The Self may also try to speak intuitively to others who could influence the outcome, but whether that works also depends on their ability to hear and respond. So an element of free will and unpredictability is built into life, which is responsible for much of the pain in the world. When bad things happen, people wonder how God could allow it, but the Self isn't always able to intervene.

Free will causes more of the suffering on the planet than events created by the Self as spiritual catalysts. That's because events caused by free will are more difficult to learn and grow from. Instead of being opportunities for learning, many events caused by free will result in setbacks to personal or spiritual growth. Sexual abuse is a good example of this. It is devastating and may take lifetimes to recover from. Sexual abuse is not an event created by the Self for growth, but it may be allowed because learning not to harm others is part of our evolution. The Self often tries to stop sexual abuse. This and many other atrocities are free-will choices that harm and set back the development and growth of many. Only more advanced souls are able to learn and grow from such events.

COMMUNICATION THROUGH THOUGHTS AND INTUITION

Just as most feelings come from the ego, so do most thoughts. The ego produces almost a constant stream of thoughts, most of which are useless or unnecessary. The Self, on the other hand, communicates through thoughts only minimally in most cases. The Self has a number of ways of communicating with us, and it doesn't use thought as much as we might assume. For the Self, thought isn't the most effective means of communicating with most people because the Self's thoughts get lost among the ego's.

Learning to distinguish the Self's thoughts from the ego's is a lesson that isn't mastered until close to the end of our lifetimes on earth. This doesn't mean the Self isn't guiding us in other ways. It is ever-present. How could it be otherwise when it *is* you?

Thoughts from the Self can be distinguished from the ego's by how they make us feel. Thoughts from the ego often leave us confused, unhappy, discontent, angry, and feeling bad about ourselves and our situation. Thoughts from the Self, on the other hand, leave us with a sense of okay-ness, that all is right with the world. They are marked by peace, love, clarity, and contentment. Clarity is one of the most obvious signs of communication from the Self because the ego rarely delivers clarity. The ego's job is to create confusion because it needs problems to solve in order to exist.

Thoughts from the Self can also be distinguished from thoughts from the ego by the energy behind the thoughts. Thoughts from the Self have the energy of a wise and caring teacher, mentor, and friend. Thoughts from the ego, on the other hand, feel tense, pushy, petty, and unkind. The ego pretends to know and states its knowledge as fact, but it is all bluster. There's no substance behind the ego, and that lack of truth can be felt. The ego's knowing is hot air, a stab at knowing, hollow advice.

Once you see this about the ego, it isn't difficult to dismiss the ego's statements, despite the certainty with which they are delivered. We learn to distrust the ego's surety; it doesn't ring true. Like a salesman, the ego tries to sell us its point of view. If that doesn't work, it tries another approach or another point of view, just like a skillful salesman. The ego behaves like a con man. It has its agenda, and it will do anything to get us to follow along.

And it is very good at it. We can learn to sense its energy of duplicity, just as we do with people.

As we evolve and learn to distinguish the Self's thoughts from the ego's, we begin to receive more thoughts from the Self because our discrimination has made the mind a more viable means of communication for the Self. The more we realize the Self is speaking to us through our thoughts and the more we listen, the more it speaks to us that way.

If we stop paying attention to the stream of communication from the ego, eventually the ego's ongoing commentary is replaced by occasional messages from the Self, which are positive, helpful, and wise. Sometimes a message is identified as coming from a particular nonphysical being, and that is called channeling. Depending on the level of the entity, the communication may be a reflection of the Self or simply another point of view, possibly not much different than the ego. Some entities serve the Self (and us), some serve themselves, and some are trying to serve us but have a limited ability to do that.

Once we are able to clearly receive thoughts from the Self, we become vulnerable to other beings who also can send thoughts into the mind, and they may not be so wise and caring, although they may pretend to be. There are many different levels of reality, from disembodied humans to aliens from other physical and nonphysical realms (all of which are actually the Self in disguise), and some don't have our best interests at heart. Like the ego, they have their own agenda, their own reason for wanting to talk with us. It may just be a power trip or for fun, but others may want to use us in some way.

Learning to discriminate between thoughts from other nonphysical beings and thoughts from the Self (or those serving the Self) is another lesson that is part of our evolution, and it can take a while to master this one. We may be fooled many times before learning to distinguish between nonphysical beings who are faking guidance and others whose work is to deliver the Self's guidance. As we evolve and awaken, that difficulty is outgrown, but the period of learning can last years and cause a lot of trouble.

The way to tell the difference between self-serving nonphysical beings and those serving the Self is by how they feel and how our Heart responds to both their energy and what they say. If what they're saying causes contraction and further ego-identification, they shouldn't be trusted. This could manifest, for example, as feeling afraid or feeling special or superior. On the other hand, if their energy and what they are saying causes feelings of expansion, openness, oneness with others, and love, they are worth listening to.

The catch is that if we are identified with the ego, we will have difficulty making this distinction. That's why meditation and other spiritual practices are recommended for those who are trying to communicate with beings in other realms. Those who try this, will reach beings who resonate with their state of consciousness: If they are identified with the ego, they will reach beings who are more self-serving; if they are identified with the Self, they will reach true helpers of the Self.

The Self communicates most directly through thoughts and intuitions. Thoughts are distinctly different from intuitions, although sometimes an intuition seems like a thought because it gets cloaked in words as soon as it is experienced. Thoughts are more tangible than intuitions. They come through as a voice in the head, which is easy to be aware of. Intuitions, on the other hand, are subtler and less defined and consequently more difficult to be aware of and trust. Intuitions are not necessarily weak, however. They may be felt very strongly, especially by those who have developed their intuition and by anyone in a critical situation that the Self is trying to reach.

Intuition is something that develops in our later lifetimes. Once we near the end of our lifetimes on earth, our intuition may feel so strong and be so trusted that we rarely ignore it. After awakening, we live mostly by our intuition because it is our connection with the Self. Thoughts, feelings, intuitions, and drives from the Self become the basis for moving through life rather than thoughts, desires, and feelings from the ego.

The shift from following the egoic mind to following the intuition is an evolutionary leap, and it makes for a very different experience of life, one that is much freer, simpler, easier, and happier. In the future, all of humanity will be living like this. Compared to what life on earth is like now, this will be heaven.

Unlike thoughts, which are experienced in the head, intuitions are felt in the body, particularly in the area around the heart. This is why it is often suggested that we follow our heart. The Heart is the Self's guidance system, which is activated as we evolve. Early in our evolution, we have little access to intuition. Only later, do we experience our intuition in a way that gets our attention.

The Heart is what connects us to the Self. It is the Self's outpost in us. When it's time for us to become aware of our divinity, the Self calls us through the Heart and awakens a longing in us to know the Self. Before that, the Self allows us to fully explore the experience of being human without much intervention from it. When it's time, the Self brings about awakening by allowing the Self to be experienced more frequently, and it does that through the Heart.

Exercise: Listening to the Self

Taking time daily to listen to the Self affirms your willingness to receive communication from the Self. Sitting quietly and listening is an invitation to the Self to speak to you.

Sit quietly and listen, as if you are expecting a very important message. Wait and listen. If you find yourself thinking, bring yourself back to listening. The Self's communication will probably not be experienced in your head. An insight might spring up in the head area, but it won't be experienced as thinking. Notice any subtle sensations in your heart area, in your gut, and in your energy field. Listen as if what you are listening for is barely audible. You may not experience an intuition, a knowing, the first time you do this, but if you continue to take time every day to listen, your ability to hear the Self will improve.

CHAPTER 8
The Heart's Wisdom

THE HEART AND SOUL

Just as the heart gives life to the human, the spiritual Heart connects us with our source and gives life to our Being. Without the Heart, we would just be a body. The Heart is what gives consciousness to the body, and it is our connection with the Self. Many call this consciousness the soul.

The soul resides in the Heart, which is located near the physical heart. It is what cycles in and out of birth, retaining the lessons and talents from each lifetime and bringing them into a new one. The soul takes on a new personality (astrology chart and other factors) every lifetime and a new life purpose, so we are unrecognizable from one lifetime to the next. However, our experiences from previous lifetimes, which are stored in the unconscious, live on in us and are often reflected in our life.

The soul is our direct link to the Self, and it has a level of materiality that can be sensed and seen by some. There are many accounts of people seeing the soul leave the body at death. Even some people who don't ordinarily see such things have reported having seen something exit the body just as someone died. The soul links the physical world with the nonphysical world and acts as a go-between.

We are used to thinking of the physical world as all that exists because that's all that our senses are able to experience. If the egoic mind can't sense something, then it can't define it, evaluate it, and take a position toward it. It doesn't like that, so it takes the position that anything that can't be sensed doesn't exist. It wishes what it can't sense and understand out of existence, but that doesn't work any more than any of its other wishes.

Nevertheless, there is something that is capable of sensing and experiencing the nonphysical world, and that is the Heart. Even those who aren't yet able to sense the nonphysical world are capable of sensing this intangible aspect of life to some extent because of the Heart, the connection to the Self.

The Self has its own sensing capabilities, which are active through the Heart. It senses, experiences, and expresses itself through the Heart. All of that is happening at the same time the ego is sensing, experiencing, and expressing itself. Both are going on simultaneously, but we usually are more aware of the ego's world than the more all-inclusive world of the Self.

The Heart has a different way of communicating to us than the ego. So if we want to know what the Heart is saying, we need to become sensitive to how it expresses itself, which is through subtle energy. This energy can be felt by anyone, but it is felt more easily by some than others, mostly because they pay more attention to it. The more attention we give to this subtle energy, the more easily it is felt. However, unless we believe this subtle dimension of life exists, we aren't likely to give it our attention. What most interferes with noticing this subtle energy is not believing it exists. Most of us are hypnotized by the ego into believing there's nothing else to sense beyond our usual senses, and yet we all do feel subtle energy. We trust the ego's viewpoint more than what we actually perceive, which is much more than what the ego perceives.

THE HEART'S WAY OF COMMUNICATING

The subtle energy of the Heart communicates by opening and closing. When we are aligned with the Self, we feel open and expansive energetically. When we are in touch with the whole of our Being, we feel expanded and complete. In contrast, when we are identified with the ego, we feel contracted, tense, and tight energetically. Being in touch with only part of who we are leaves us feeling small and separate.

This sense of smallness manifests not only energetically, but also emotionally: We feel vulnerable, afraid, weak, incapable, inadequate, unworthy, and lacking. These feelings result in behaving defensively toward life. Because the *me* is seen as separate and in peril, we feel we have to look out for it. Others and the world in general are perceived as threatening to the ego, and that makes not only our energy tense and tight, but also our physical body.

Because we feel like something is missing and we don't like how that feels, we become focused on trying to get rid of that feeling. Well, something *is* missing: awareness of the entirety of our Being. When we lose touch with the truth of who we are, we do feel small, and rightfully so. However, just as losing sight of something doesn't make it go away, losing sight of who we are doesn't make the Self go away. It's there even when we aren't sensing it.

Once we are aware of this energetic opening and closing, we can use it to realign with the Self: When we feel contracted, that means we aren't aligned. What is responsible? Whatever we are thinking. The sense of contraction, which may manifest physically as tightness and emotionally as feeling bad, is a sign that what we are giving our attention to is not the whole truth, not the entire picture. When we give our attention to everything that is present in the moment, we feel expanded, connected to life, free, content, and happy. When we don't feel free, content, and happy, that means we have given our attention to only a small part of what is present in the moment: a thought, a desire, or a feeling.

When we give a thought our attention, we become identified with it; we get lost in it. Becoming identified with a thought is like diving into it, becoming immersed in it, and forgetting everything else. If that thought isn't the whole truth (and no thought ever is), then we are immersing ourselves in a partial truth, a lie. And that will cause us to suffer, no matter what that thought is. Suffering is a red flag that shows us we are identified with the ego. Realigning with the Self happens simply by seeing that we have given our attention to too small a part of what is present in the moment and then giving our attention to more of what is present.

The moment has a lot to it. A thought or feeling is often part of the moment, but any moment has much more to it than thoughts and feelings. When we give our attention to a thought or feeling and become identified with it, we miss the rest of what is present in the moment, such as peace, love, contentment, and acceptance, a great feeling of okay-ness. We also may miss any insight, guidance, or inspiration to act that the Self may be communicating, not to mention the pleasure of the senses and the pleasure of just being alive. We identify with the thought or feeling as if it is all that exists in that moment, but the moment offers much more than that.

Exercise: Giving Your Attention to the Moment

This inquiry will help you include more in your awareness than just your thoughts and feelings.

What is coming out of the moment right now? Notice how the egoic mind wants to pull you away from whatever is happening in the moment with a story about the past, about what is happening now, or about the future. The egoic mind tells stories. It puts a spin on every experience. Notice that, and then notice what else is coming out of the moment. What else is present in your awareness right now besides your thoughts? You are never done noticing what is present because what is present is always changing. The experience of what is present is very rich, very alive, and very nourishing, no matter what is happening or not happening, unlike the egoic mind's stories.

Thoughts and feelings are not a problem if we don't give all our attention to them. If we notice *everything* that is present in our awareness, not just the thought or feeling, the thought or feeling won't feel like a problem. It won't be seen as something you need to do something about, but just something that happens to be arising. Although some thoughts are useful and acting on them might be appropriate, most thoughts are useless and don't enhance our experience of life. Once we begin living from a deeper place, a place that is more aligned with the Self, the uselessness of our thoughts becomes obvious, and we only give our attention to thoughts when thinking is relevant.

For example, let's say the thought "I need to lose weight" arises. This is a common thought that may arise countless times in one day. With any thought, it's helpful to ask: "Is it true?" The answer in this case, as with most thoughts, is no because it isn't the whole truth. With many thoughts, like this one, we often have to look deeper to what that thought implies to see why it isn't true.

It may be true that losing weight is a good idea, but the thought "I need to lose weight" implies something more than this, such as, "I need to lose weight to feel better about myself" or "I need to lose weight to attract a mate" or "I need to lose weight to be better looking." None of those thoughts are true. They assume something that isn't true. Feeling good about ourselves, attracting a mate, or being better looking are not contingent on losing weight except in the universe created by the ego. These are just the stories the ego is telling about the *me*. The story changes nearly every moment, as the ego comes up with other assumptions, lies, about what the *me* needs to be happier, more loved, better looking, and whatever else it wants.

Usually what we do when a thought like this arises is latch onto it and engage the mind in problem-solving: We do a lot of thinking. In this case, you think about losing weight: You think of ways you've tried to lose weight in the past. You fantasize about what will happen if you do lose weight. You imagine what will happen if you don't. You think about what so-and-so said about losing weight. You think about how others in your family dealt with their weight and yours in the past. You think about how hard it is to lose weight. You think about how you've failed in the past.

And then the feelings begin to arise: You *feel bad* about yourself for not being thin, you are *afraid* of what will happen if you don't lose weight, you are *jealous* of people who are thin, you *hate* being fat! Now you really do have a problem because you don't want to feel that way. So you engage the mind again in a specific plan, and around and around you go, generating more thoughts and feelings. Meanwhile, what else is happening in the present moment?

Now let's go back to the possibility that it might be a good idea to lose weight. If that idea comes from the Self and is not co-opted by the ego, steps will be taken in that direction, and it won't generate a lot of thinking. It will just feel true, and you will do something about it. You can probably think of times when that happened, when you just dropped a habit because you were done with it, without a lot of struggle, internal arguments, or thought. This isn't usually the case with habits, but it does happen. The reason that habits aren't changed this easily more often is that the ego takes over and tries to manage the situation in its own way.

When we are aligned with the Self, there's an ease about being in the world. We have a clear vision of what needs to be done, and we don't waste time on imaginary problems. We're free of the complications of the ego's conflicting advice, information, opinions, and judgments. The ego doesn't know how to meet challenges and solve problems, so it makes a stab at every possible solution. Confusion and indecision are its hallmarks, and they are a sure sign that we are identified with the ego and not the Self.

Sometimes problems do need to be solved and decisions made. Let's take the example of moving: A desire to move arises from the Self. Perhaps there is something in another location that will benefit its plan. However, where to move and how to do that may not be apparent immediately. There is often quite a time lag between the Self's inspiration to do something and the details of how to do it. During that time lag, the egoic mind gets very busy trying to figure out the solution: It researches, talks to people, makes lists, and thinks and thinks and thinks some more, as if thinking will produce the answer more quickly. However, every decision of the Self has its own timing. When the Self is ready to reveal the answer, it will, and it may or may not coincide with the decision arrived at by thinking.

On the other hand, if the idea to move is the ego's, perhaps out of general discontentment and the belief that you would be happier elsewhere, the decision will probably be made by the ego as well. As long as it doesn't interfere with the Self's plan, the Self will allow you to follow the ego's ideas.

The ego causes us to be much busier than we need to be. In its search for happiness, it comes up with one scheme after another, plans the details, and executes them. These experiences are all grist for the mill of our evolution, but they don't necessarily lead to a happier, more fulfilled life. This is one reason living from the Self is much easier than living from the ego.

The Self allows us to follow the ego's schemes because making choices and experiencing the consequences of those choices is integral to our evolution. By making choices and trying out things that don't make us happy, we discover what does make us happy. Only after lifetimes of experience with choosing do we make the ultimate choice of the Self over the ego (which has to be made again in each new moment) and become so aligned with the Self that we only do what fulfills us and not what doesn't fulfill us. That leaves us with a lot more time and energy to put into what really matters.

FOLLOWING YOUR HEART

The ego communicates through the mind; the Self communicates through the Heart. In any moment, both are occurring simultaneously. In any moment, we have a choice: Follow the egoic mind or follow the Heart. This is somewhat complicated by the fact that the Self sometimes communicates through the mind, and the mind is needed to handle practical matters, such as making a grocery list and following a recipe. However, for how to live life, the egoic mind is a terrible guide. The trouble is we are so conditioned to using the mind for everything, including guidance, that we may not realize that something else is guiding us.

For most people, the egoic mind runs their activities most of the time, and the Self steps in only occasionally and steers life. As we evolve, we become more aware of the Self being active in our lives, and we begin to allow the Self to guide us more frequently. Eventually, we join with the Self consciously, instead of identifying with the ego.

To be identified with the ego takes a certain amount of unconsciousness, or lack of awareness and critical examination of what is going on in the mind and in the moment. The ability to be aware of our thoughts and to be present in the moment increases as we evolve, and that eventually enables us to see through the false self and to align with something else.

We have to see through the illusion of the false self to some extent before we realize that the Self exists. Until then, we are somewhat at the mercy of the egoic mind, which takes us on one wild goose chase after another. Finally, when we have suffered enough, we begin to wonder why we are suffering and what life is all about.

Answers to questions like these can only be found in the Heart. The ego doesn't know what life is all about. That's not the ego's job, even if it pretends to know. The ego is meant to be a tool of the Self, but like a Frankenstein monster, the ego has taken over. This takeover is part of the drama intentionally created by the Self out of curiosity to see what will happen. The Self also intends for that monster to be subdued, so the Self's plan also includes a happy ending. Like a dream that the Self is enjoying, it knows it will wake up from it. But for the time being, it will explore the possibilities within the illusion.

The mind can take us to the edge of the Self's territory, but it can't cross the threshold. For that, we need the Heart. It is the bridge to the Self, and it's what allows us to experience who we really are. However, the Heart doesn't operate like the mind; the Heart is wordless. It communicates energetically, through sensations of openness and contraction. These sensations are the yes-no code of the Heart: When the Heart says yes, we feel open, expansive, and connected to the Whole. When the Heart says no, we feel contracted, tight, and small.

The simplest way to communicate with the Heart, then, is by asking yes-no questions and then waiting for a response energetically. For instance, you might ask the Heart if moving to a particular place is right for you at this time. If you feel expansive, that is a yes; if you feel contracted, that is a no. However, there's a catch: The answer only holds true in that moment. So if you are asking about something that has long-range consequences, such as a move, you need to ask the question repeatedly over time. This is because factors that play into any decision are constantly changing, so the answer could change if any of those factors changes.

Asking yes-no questions of the Heart and noticing the response is a simple way to practice getting a feel for the Heart's way of communicating. This method of inquiry can be applied to every moment's experience, particularly to a thought, to see just how true it is. You can tell if a thought is coming from the Self or from the ego by sensing how it affects you energetically. Whenever you think a thought, it's followed by an energetic response: an expansive feeling, contraction, or something in between that could be considered neutral. Many thoughts are simply neutral. They are usually the more factual ones, such as, "The pen is blue." The truth of all other thoughts can be tested by observing their effect on you energetically.

Although factual thoughts are neutral, they are often followed by a judgmental thought, such as, "I don't like blue pens," which will cause contraction, however subtle, because it comes from the ego, not the Self. Most thoughts that start with "I" come from the ego and not the Self. They reflect only a small truth, the ego's truth. If you notice, you will see that most of your thoughts, except the factual ones, start with "I."

Reactions to thoughts cover a range from weak to stong. "I don't like blue pens" would not cause the level of contraction that "I wish I were dead" would. With many thoughts, especially thoughts that aren't associated with feelings, the contraction is faint. Thoughts associated with feelings, such as "I hate myself," tend to result in more noticeable contractions. Even a positive thought, such as, "That was brilliant of me," is likely to cause some contraction because positive thoughts about the *me* separate us from others just as much as negative ones, and separation equals suffering.

The farther away we get from our true nature, the smaller and more contracted we feel, and the more we suffer. This suffering is designed to wake us up out of ego-identification and point us back to the Self, to what is true. So for example, if you are thinking that you can't do anything right, you will feel contracted and bad. These negative feelings can be a reminder to you that what you just thought must be coming from the ego and therefore not very true. All it takes to get back in alignment with the Self is seeing the falseness of what you just thought.

Once we see the ego's lies, they lose their power to affect our feelings and actions. On the other hand, if we believe a lie, we will go down the path of contraction and further ego-identification: We will feel bad and then try to think our way out of feeling bad, or we will do something to try to feel better, such as eat or drink too much or do something that is irrelevant to the Self's plan. That is how the ego can derail us from the Self's plan. The Self allows that to happen because its plan is very flexible and adaptable to our choices, and every choice results in some kind of learning.

Because every moment is different, this test of how true a thought is needs to be applied again and again. Testing out every thought could keep us very busy. So fortunately, there's a shortcut: You only need to apply this test when you are suffering. Suffering is a sign that we are believing the ego. Factual thoughts and the ones we don't believe aren't a problem; they just come and go because we don't get caught up in them. However, some thoughts catch us up, usually ones that carry a strong judgment about the *me*. Those are the ones most likely to draw us into ego-identification. Judgments about others and other things have the same effect, but usually those judgments don't grab us quite as strongly as judgments about ourselves.

Absorption with the *me* is behind much of our suffering not only because the *me* is a very small part of the present moment, but also because the *me* doesn't even exist. It isn't real. Constant self-reflection seems valuable when we are engaged in it. We believe that thinking about ourselves and our life is a way of improving our life, but instead, these thoughts take us away from life.

When we forget for a moment about the *me*, we still exist as consciousness. This consciousness is moving the body and aware of everything there is to be aware of. The *me* doesn't need to be in the picture at all for life to be happening. The experience of no *me* is quite surprising when we first begin experiencing it for longer periods of time, but really, it is the most natural state. What could be more natural than just being, just responding from moment to moment to what is arising?

The ego doesn't trust this way of being. It believes it has to figure out every moment ahead of time, or it won't get it right. The ego plans future moments and evaluates past moments, but what about the present moment? The ego is too busy thinking to notice the present moment. The present moment is perfect just the way it is, but the ego won't be convinced of that. It's certain it knows how to make the present moment better. Meanwhile, the moments are ticking away, unnoticed. Beingness, the smells, the birds chirping, the breeze, the sun's warmth, the play of light, the beauty, the richness of being alive—all this and so much more is being missed. The ego has more important things to do.

There's a choice to be made. The choice is to follow your thoughts or follow your Heart. The Self will let you follow your thoughts forever if you like, but you won't want to. Identifying with your thoughts just doesn't make you feel good, and all that running around doesn't bring you happiness. Eventually, we find this out. Our drive to be someone fizzles because we see that the ego's striving doesn't work, and it exacts a toll on our happiness. Trying to be someone is exhausting: We never get to rest, we never have enough, we never are enough, and we never arrive. Real happiness is in just being, without being anyone and without thinking anything. That is where happiness lies. It has always been available in the space between our thoughts.

QUIETING THE MIND

Intuition is the language of the Heart. The Self speaks to us primarily through our intuition. It uses other methods of communication as well, but intuition is to the Heart, what thoughts are to the mind. Intuitions flow nearly constantly, like thoughts, but becoming aware of intuitions takes some practice because they are much subtler than thoughts. For that reason, thoughts usually win our attention over intuitions.

One of the benefits of meditation and other spiritual practices that quiet the egoic mind is that these practices make intuition more accessible. Most people need meditation or some other spiritual practice to subdue the dominance of the egoic mind. Once some mastery of the egoic mind is achieved, real progress can be made toward following our intuition.

Meditation, or any other activity that focuses the mind, causes the egoic mind to become quiet because it keeps the mind busy with a task. Actually, any activity we are fully engaged in can serve as a meditation. When we focus all of our attention on something, the mind becomes quiet and serves us only when needed.

We tend to skim by on the surface of life, instead of diving into the moment and really experiencing it. The egoic mind keeps us at a distance from the real experience and, instead, substitutes thoughts *about* the experience. It distances us from the present moment, where life is rich and alive. We can learn to be more present to the moment by just noticing what is going on. Being more present is usually accomplished by taking our attention off of thoughts and feelings and putting it on whatever else is happening in the moment.

Exercise: Being Present

This is a practice for every moment, no matter what the circumstances.

Being present means giving your attention to everything that is happening in the moment, not just to your thoughts or feelings. If a thought arises, notice it, and then continue to notice everything else that is present. When you are engaged in a task and your mind wanders off of it, bring your attention back to the task, to the sensations that are present, and to the entire experience of that moment. With practice, being present to everything that's going on in the moment will become more natural.

Doing a more formal kind of meditation is another very helpful practice. When done on a regular basis, meditation helps establish a calm mental state, which makes the intuition and consequently the Self's guidance more accessible. Meditation is the most effective spiritual technique available for shifting out of the egoic state of consciousness and into the experience of our true nature. It is also no more complicated or difficult than being present to an activity.

Exercise: Sitting in Meditation

Make a commitment to meditate daily, even if you only do it for a few minutes a day. Start by meditating for ten minutes a day. Increase the amount of time you meditate as your enjoyment of it increases. Be sure to make your experience of meditation as comfortable, enjoyable, and pleasant as possible so that you look forward to meditating.

Retreat to a quiet place. Choose something to focus on that you enjoy so that your meditation will be pleasurable. If you are auditory, you would probably enjoy listening to music or to the sounds in the room. If you are more kinesthetic, you would probably enjoy focusing on any physical sensations and on any subtle energetic sensations that are present. If you are more visual, you might enjoy gazing at a picture of a saint, a work of art, colors, flowers, or something in nature.

Whenever your mind wanders, gently bring it back to what you are focusing on. Also notice what you are experiencing as you sit in meditation. While the mind is busy with what it's focusing on, experience is still happening. That experience is who you are! As you practice meditation more, your mind will wander less and for shorter periods of time, and you will spend increasing amounts of time in the Now.

Once you begin spending more time in the Now, meditation becomes very pleasurable. The now is intensely pleasurable. It has everything: joy, bliss, peace, contentment, fulfillment, love, clarity, acceptance, and wisdom. You will wonder why you ever wandered from the Now, but then you will catch yourself doing it again. The egoic mind is very seductive, even though the Now is so joyous and full. Even those who live mostly in the Now find themselves wandering through the corridors of the egoic mind from time to time.

We can learn to be present to the thoughts in our egoic mind just as we are present to whatever else might be arising in any moment. Thinking can be like any other activity we are present to. When we are present to our thoughts, we don't feel like we are thinking them, but more like we are noticing them being thought, which is very different from the usual way of thinking. Here is an exercise that will help you learn to be present to your thoughts:

Exercise: Being Present to Thoughts

Practicing being present to your thoughts will change your relationship to thought. Practice this as much as possible whenever thoughts arise.

Notice whatever thought is arising right now. Observe it as if you were standing at a distance from it. What is the experience of thinking? Notice that thinking seems to be contained in your head. What is aware of thinking? Is that Awareness contained by anything, even your body? How big is it? Does it have a boundary? What is the experience of this Awareness? That is who you are. You are the Awareness that is aware of thoughts coming and going.

The thoughts that arise in your egoic mind have nothing to do with who you really are. What arises in your egoic mind is not up to you. It is just the conditioning you were given. Without following a thought, commenting on a thought, or holding an opinion about a thought, simply observe how your thoughts come and go: One thought replaces another. Where do they come from? Where do they go? Notice how little coherence there is between thoughts and how they jump from subject to subject. At times, it seems they are designed solely to get your attention. What else do you notice about them? Are there different voices attached to them? Do you notice certain themes? How true are they? Do they have an impact on Awareness?

Being present to thoughts this way allows us to be objective about them. With objectivity, we can examine our thoughts in a way that wasn't possible when we were identified with them. Through such an examination, a great deal can be learned about the nature of our conditioning, and what we learn about our conditioning can free us from it.

This new relationship to the egoic mind is very freeing. It not only can free us from our conditioning, but also free us to be aware of the fullness of the moment. Because the egoic mind no longer has the power to draw us into identification, we are free to give our attention to the whole of life, instead of to only our thoughts. What we discover is that part of what is happening in the whole of life is that the Self is speaking to us in its own way, through intuition.

COMMUNICATING WITH THE SELF

Communing with the Self is a much more positive experience than communing with the egoic mind. Instead of feeling separate, we feel connected to who we are and to all of life. This results in feeling less afraid, less defensive, less needy, and less restless than when we are busy with our mental dialogues. Communing with the Self feels like coming home. We feel safe, nurtured, loved, and accepted, which is the opposite of how the egoic mind makes us feel. Furthermore, we receive the guidance we need to live life spontaneously and happily.

Now that you are sold on the value of communing with the Self, you probably want to know how to do it. The good news is you are already communing with the Self, but you might not be aware of the Self's communication as much as you could be if you are giving most of your attention to your thoughts.

When our attention is on our thoughts, it can't be on what the Self is communicating because we can't give our attention to two things at once, although our attention can go back and forth between two things in a millisecond. If you can only give your attention to one thing at a time, what will it be? Your thoughts and feelings, or everything else that is happening in the moment? When we give our attention fully to the moment, we are guided to think when we need to. We think when thinking is needed, and act when acting is needed. Thinking and acting, or just being, spring naturally from the moment.

Whatever springs from the moment is the Self acting in our life. The Self communicates its intentions through impulses to act. These impulses are the primary way the Self guides us. Intuitions can turn so immediately into actions that we don't realize that an intuition to act came first. Our intuition works spontaneously like this most of the time.

More commonly, we experience an intuition as a download of information or as a knowing that bubbles up and may become cloaked in words and then thought about. Thinking about an intuition is not a problem if those thoughts don't interfere with following the intuition. But often an intuition is shelved because the egoic mind discounts it or disagrees with it. Another possibility is that the egoic mind distorts the intuition and takes action that is very different from what was intended.

Once we are aware of what intuitions feel like, we can catch them before the egoic mind dismisses or misinterprets them. Because intuitions feel very different from thoughts, they are easy to recognize. And the more we become aware of them, the easier they are to recognize.

Intuitions are more like feelings and sensations than thoughts. Intuitions arrive in the body, particularly in the chest area, instead of in the head. At first, intuitions can be quite faint, but when we become more sensitive to them, they can be very compelling and so strong and distinct that their meaning is unmistakable. An intuition may feel like a fist in the chest that doesn't go away until we follow it.

When it's time to begin to awaken, our intuition becomes stronger, and the Self makes the benefits of listening to it more apparent by showing us what happens if we don't. This is how the Self teaches us to be more attentive to our intuition, and that tactic works. We do start paying more attention to it because we see that our intuition can save us from trouble and even tragedy. Because of this advantage to our survival, the ego is willing to allow some exploration and development of the intuition. Once we get a taste of living from our intuition, however, we begin to become disenchanted with the ego, and the illusion starts to unravel. Listening to our intuition moves us toward awakening and away from ego-identification. This is one way the Self drives evolution toward itself and away from the ego.

CHAPTER 9
Ready or Not, You're It

THE ROLE OF FREE WILL IN CREATION

The Self has a plan for earth and for all of creation, including a plan for you. You and your plan are part of a vision for the evolution of all of creation. We can intuit elements of that vision at times, but because of the immensity of this greater plan, we can't fully grasp it. Nor does the Self know exactly how its plan will unfold. Just as the Self has only so much control over each of our plans, it has only so much control over how all of creation will unfold. Nevertheless, because the Self isn't separate from creation, the Self is able to affect creation enough to guide it in the direction that the Self intends.

Although the Self's will ultimately determines the destiny of creation, free will is built into creation. What would be the point of creating something that was entirely predictable? The joy of creating is in discovering what that creation is capable of. Isn't that the joy you have in creating a child or anything else? If you invent something, for instance, the joy is in discovering what that invention can do, where its limits are, how it might be used or misused, and what effect it will have on everything else.

A creator creates not only to fulfill a need, but also for the joy of experimentation. This is the joy the artist has in creating as well: "What if I put this color here and this one there?" Just as we love to create and explore by creating, so does the Self. Much of the creating we do is inspired by the Self: The Self creates us, and then it continues to create through us.

The Self spins off parts of itself into different forms and gives them a separate consciousness, which makes free will possible. Without a sense of being separate, free will would not be possible. We must feel separate and believe we are separate in order to act as if we are, or our actions would still reflect the Self. The Self can only separate itself from creation through an illusion because if everything is the Self, how could the Self not be aware of itself?

Free will is real. We do have the ability to make choices. A number of factors influence those choices, however. Our astrology chart plays a big part in determining our choices, as does our family and cultural conditioning. Because of all these influences on our behavior, free will is not that free. For instance, if you have an Aries Moon, you are not that free to not express your feelings. That moon sign makes feelings difficult to contain.

It is said that character is destiny, and the character you have chosen to play in this lifetime, based on your astrology chart and other factors, will have strong tendencies to behave in certain ways and to make certain choices. We are programmed with particular traits and tendencies, and our free will acts within those parameters most of the time.

Our free will can also be influenced by the Self. It has ways of influencing us to choose what it wants. For example, if you decide to move somewhere that would interfere with the Self's plan, it can create obstacles to discourage you. If that doesn't work, it can create difficulties once you move that might cause you to rethink your choice. Some of the difficulties we experience aren't just part of life or due to karma, but are due to the Self's attempt to shape our decisions. One way the Self communicates its intentions is through difficulties.

In the same way, the Self may make certain choices easier if those choices suit its plan. For example, if your plan would benefit from a move to a certain location, the Self is likely to ease the way to moving there. It would convey the idea to move there intuitively to you or through someone else and then it may provide the means and other things that would increase the appeal of that move.

So free will is not as free as we might think. Furthermore, as we evolve, our intuition becomes so strong that our personal will becomes aligned with the Self's, and going against the Self no longer feels like an option. And why would we go against the Self, when life runs so smoothly with the Self at the helm? In a sense, this ease is the reward for all the difficult lessons that resulted from exercising our free will in the past, since free will generally means the ego's will. We eventually graduate from free will and the difficulties caused by it to following the Self's will and the happiness, peace, and contentment in that.

As a result of free will, creation can get pretty messy. Free will causes a lot of problems and a lot of suffering. We pay a big price for this freedom. The best we can hope for when we are identified with the ego and exercising free will is to express the ego's will positively instead of negatively.

THE GLOBAL PLAN

Free will can be a problem for the Self during critical times, when it is necessary to drive evolution in a certain direction. Just as the Self may create difficulties to point us in a certain direction, it may create difficulties on a global level to steer our choices. It will use every method possible to move its plan forward as intended.

Some of the difficulties we are experiencing in the world are karmic. They are the result of previous actions, sometimes of other generations and other times. Others are created by the Self to move the world in another direction. However, most of the problems and suffering in the world today are caused by a misguided use of free will.

Ego-identification can't help but cause suffering not only on an individual level, but also on a global level, particularly when someone with power is ego-identified. Until we have enlightened (awake) leaders, the world will continue to experience war and atrocities. Unenlightened leaders demonstrate what ego-identification combined with power is capable of, and we all learn from the actions of unenlightened leaders through the suffering caused by their actions.

Waking up is the most important thing you can do to help the world. All the evil and suffering in the world is a result of ego-identification, which keeps us tied to our conditioning and limits our ability to give our time and energy to more fulfilling things, to our life purpose. We all need to fulfill our life purpose so that the greater plan can unfold as intended.

COMMITMENT TO THE TRUTH

The hardest thing about waking up is staying committed to the Truth and not getting pulled back into the illusion. We have to want the Truth more than we want to be someone, more than we want to be a *me* with a story. Until we fully commit ourselves to the Truth, the ego will remain in charge. The ego has every reason to resist our awakening, but the suffering of ego-identification ultimately wakes us up. The ego is both the problem and the solution. Given this, we can't help but wake up, eventually.

Seeing through the ego's games is important. However, seeing through the illusion is not quite enough. Many go back to sleep after seeing the Truth because they are comfortable in their old identities, in their story of *me*. Even if their story of *me* causes them suffering, they like being a *me* who struggles and suffers and wants. They like the drama of their story, and they tell and retell it to whoever will listen. They enjoy their suffering, until they don't.

It takes commitment to the Truth, not just seeing the Truth, to stay awake for increasing amounts of time. Once our commitment is strong enough, we don't go back to sleep. Many live in a quasi-dreamland, that state between sleeping and waking, moving in and out of illusion for a long time before the commitment is made.

Where does that commitment come from? If it isn't there, we can't fake it. It's either there or not. Many suffer over not having enough commitment, but that's just more suffering over the way things are. If what *is*, is that your commitment isn't strong enough yet, accepting that is the only course for now. When the time comes to be awake and stay awake, your commitment will strengthen. The Self determines when that will be. You, the ego, are powerless to determine that, just as *you* have been powerless to determine anything.

There's a time for everything. Those who have come here to wake up and to wake others up are awakened by the Self when the time is right. When awakening will happen, no one knows, but when it does happen, it will be undeniable. Spiritual seekers suffer so much over wanting to wake up and not being able to. When we are identified with the ego, we want to awaken because we want to feel better. But that motivation isn't good enough because that desire to awaken is still about *me*, about getting a better *me* and a better life for *me*. People want a way out of the suffering caused by the egoic mind, but most don't really want to lose their egoic mind. They are still attached to it and to their conditioning. They still believe what the egoic mind says. They still believe they are who their thoughts tell them they are.

Many want to wake up, but they don't want to pay the price. It seems very dear: The *me* and its story. But how hard is it, really, to give up something that doesn't even exist? If you didn't have a Lexus, would it be hard to give it up? Of course not. But if you believed you had a Lexus, it would be. To awaken, all you need to do is stop believing in something that doesn't exist. Nothing else changes, really, just the belief that *you* exist, that *you* matter. The truth stays the same: *You* never existed in the first place. It was all an illusion.

This truth can be hard to swallow. It means giving up not only our ideas about ourselves, but all our ideas: all our opinions, beliefs, judgments, hopes, dreams, fantasies, desires, and our ideas about the past and future. These ideas are what make us who we think we are. Nothing else. These ideas are all that have ever differentiated us from others, us from the Self. This may seem like a high price, but what are we giving up, really? They are just ideas. They are less substantial than air, which at least we can experience. We can't experience any of our ideas about ourselves or about the world. They exist only in the mind, where they were created and where they eventually return.

The egoic mind is the great generator of identity. It is a master at generating ideas about who we are, and none of them are real. What is real about the concept of mother, for instance? It's a useful label in conversing with others, but it has no substance. We can touch someone who calls herself a mother, but we can't touch a mother. All our roles and identities are like this. They are just ideas dreamed up by the ego, a way of thinking the false self into reality.

We can just as easily make the false self disappear by *not* thinking. When we stop thinking, our story about *me* disappears. This is proof that the *me* is a fabrication of the egoic mind. When we stop thinking, or even just stop paying attention to our thoughts, the *me* disappears. In its place, is the truth of who we are, the Self, which can't be put into words.

The Self has been here all along. It is the only thing that has ever been here, and you are it! What a great surprise it is to discover that everywhere you look, there you are. This discovery makes you want to look and look and look some more. The joy with which the Self views creation is indescribable. Why would we ever turn away from that joy? You don't have to. Everything you need to be exquisitely happy is right here. You don't have to do a thing but be who you really are and be it fully without distraction, without a thought of anything else. You *are* the Beloved you have been searching for, for so long.

ABOUT THE AUTHOR

Gina Lake is a spiritual teacher who is devoted to helping others wake up and live in the Now through counseling, intensives, and her books. She has a masters degree in counseling psychology and over twenty years experience supporting people in their spiritual growth. Her books include *Radical Happiness, Embracing the Now, Anatomy of Desire, Return to Essence, What About Now? Loving in the Moment, Living in the Now,* and *Getting Free.* Her website offers information about her books and consultations, free e-books, book excerpts, a free monthly newsletter, a blog, and audio and video recordings: *www.radicalhappiness.com.*

4785472

Made in the USA
Lexington, KY
02 March 2010